HOW TO BECOME

A

MILLIONAIRE

BY

SLOW SPENDING

A personal financial journey

Dr Ranjan Sharma and Ms Mary Sharma

First publication 2026

National Library of Australia Cataloguing-in-Publication data:

Sharma, Ranjan & Sharma, Mary

How to Become a Millionaire by Slow Spending

ISBN 978-1-7648945-2-4

Table of Contents

Dedicated to our beautiful, kind and resourceful mothers who are no longer with us and who instilled frugality in us

Ellen McSwiney

Vimla Sharma

Preface

Why we authored this book?

There are hundreds of books on the topic of becoming a millionaire. Some of the authors are well regarded and are themselves multi-millionaires. There are also number of strategies such as investing shares and property investment for becoming millionaire. Many of these require leverage of funds from financial institutions as strategies for investments. As we come from middle class families with no financial background, we lacked the courage and strategies that were promoted by others. Also, we started earning money quite late (31 and 28 years) in our lives as we were both busy in getting education (BSc, MSc, PhD and MBA).

Without following any specific strategy, but rather following a combination of steps, over 20+ years, we have been successful in becoming millionaires and we have decided to share our experience here. We think our experience will be valuable for others from middle class, especially, if they start to follow our strategies from early stages of life, which revolve around constantly reducing and optimising spending, a strategy we call "**Slow Spending**".

Our financial journey really started when we moved to Australia in February 2001. At the age of 38 and 35, we moved to Australia from Denmark, with some cash that we had saved, but with no intention of becoming millionaires. When we got to Australia, our aim was simply to own our own home, raise family and save some money on the side for rainy days and regular travel back to our folks in India and Ireland. Along the way, we were frugal, bought and sold some properties, got lucky in getting decent jobs and somehow created a financial security for us. It took us many years, and we took some steps inadvertently that fuelled our financial success. In this book we have tried to dig deep into what has happened that has led to our financial freedom.

In 2025, at the age of 61, when Ranjan decided to stop working and found plenty of spare time, we decided to put together our story so that others could benefit from our simple strategies.

We believe there is a unique recipe for becoming a millionaire within each one of us. How we go about finding and optimising that recipe depends on each one of us. How we are brought up, how we educate ourselves, how we earn and spend, will determine how we go about becoming millionaires. Perhaps, this book will encourage others to follow strategies like ours and find themselves becoming financially independent and enjoying the life the way we are.

Summary

Getting financial freedom in life is a sweet goal that we all strive for. We would all like to be millionaires, however, circumstances may not allow us to achieve those goals. In this book, after analysing our own life trajectory, we have systematically outlined the steps one can take to become a millionaire. This process that we have used, we call it "**Slow Spending**". Slow spending refers to constantly reducing the rate of spending with respect to the rate of income. In a mathematical term, we are constantly reducing the slope of the "time versus spending" curve in life. We believe that each one of us have potential to become a millionaire by using the slow spending tricks as suggested in this book.

Slow spending as a pathway to become a millionaire requires financial discipline for over 10-20 years or more after gaining a steady source of income such as an employment or business. The duration of the pathways depends on one's ability to earn, sacrifice, save and invest. Many other factors also play important roles such as market conditions, growth of assets etc. In this book, we outline our experience and strategy over 25+ years mainly through a small portfolio of properties.

We believe that the life is life a **Swiss army knife** and it has many opportunities, like the various tools on the knife, to save money in numerous ways, and create a habit of "**Slow Spending**" to become a millionaire!

Our pathway to become millionaires is through sacrifice, slow, systematic savings and investments without compromising our lifestyle. For us, having money is a mean to an end. The end for us is to have meaningful relationships, contributing to the society and to achieve financial freedom.

Over the period 25+ years, we have bought and sold several properties and made several mistakes. What has kept us financially growing was our ability to spend significantly lower than our income, *i.e.* **slow spending**, and getting rid of loans obtained for investment properties. It has not been easy, but it has not been that hard. We have enjoyed the journey and had opportunities to travel around the world. The journey has led us to our current financial position where can comfortably live with returns without diluting our capital.

Some people believe that reaching a million dollars is hard and, it is too low an amount to be wealthy and do not bother to put efforts to get there. On the other hand, we believe, if you get to a million dollar by sacrificing and "**slow spending**" it becomes lot easier to attain further millions, as along the way, you learn so much about earning, saving, investing and spending that you find your unique ways of reaching financial freedom.

This book is aimed at ordinary folks who are born in middle class, have little or no financial background and but are keen to learn from our methodology. Although we have lived most of our lives in Australia and based some of the research on Australian data, we believe the general principles of "**Slow Spending**" apply anywhere in the world.

We have first defined what slow spending is and what are the various means of achieving slow spending. We have then followed up with our journey to achieve financial freedom through **slow spending**.

Although we started our financial journey quite late in our lives (age 38 and 35), we believe that younger you start, easier it is to become a millionaire and achieve that financial freedom in life. The good old strategy of compounding is real benefit if you start early in life. We believe, it is a combination of habits that you develop over time that helps in developing strategies for earning, saving and investing opportunities.

Although we started our financial journey quite late in [illegible] lives (age 32 and 35), I believe that you [illegible] [illegible]

An introduction to our life journey

Our Life Journey: From Humble Beginnings to Financial Freedom

Roots in Two Continents

We are Ranjan and Mary, two ordinary souls whose paths converged in an extraordinary tale of love, adventure, and financial independence. Our story begins on opposite sides of the globe, in the vibrant landscapes of India and the rolling green hills of Ireland. Born into middle-class families with no particular emphasis on wealth or financial strategies, we were shaped by simplicity, hard work, and a shared dream of building a meaningful life together.

Ranjan's journey began in a remote village nestled in the foothills of the Himalayas in northern India. Life there was simple, surrounded by the rugged beauty of mountains and the rhythm of rural existence. His parents, a schoolteacher and a nurse, raised five children on modest means, instilling values of frugality and perseverance. Education was Ranjan's ticket to a broader world. After completing his schooling, he earned a place at a prestigious dairy science and technology program in Gujarat, a state on India's western coast known for its agricultural innovation. The bustling energy of Gujarat was a stark contrast to his quiet village, and it sparked a curiosity that would define his future.

After graduating, Ranjan briefly worked for a dairy company in Punjab, immersing himself in the industry. But his ambition stretched further. He secured a coveted scholarship from the Indian Council of Agricultural Research (ICAR) to pursue a master's degree back in Gujarat. There, his passion for food science deepened, and he began to dream of studying for PhD abroad. With determination and a touch of boldness, he applied to universities worldwide and after receiving many rejections, was thrilled to receive an offer from Massey University in New Zealand for a PhD in food science. In June 1989, Ranjan stepped off a plane in Palmerston North, a small but vibrant town, ready to embark on a new chapter. A few months later, his dedication paid off when he was awarded the prestigious New Zealand Vice Chancellor's research scholarship, cementing his place in the research world.

Mary's story unfolded across the ocean in Midleton, a charming small town in County Cork, Ireland. Raised in a close-knit family, she grew up with the warmth of Irish community life. Her father worked at a local refinery, while her mother managed the home, caring for Mary and her three siblings. Like Ranjan's family, the household was modest, with no focus on financial planning but a strong emphasis on living simply and valuing what they had.

Mary's sharp mind and love for learning led her to pursue a master's degree in food science, a field that combined her curiosity about the natural world with her desire to make a difference.

Her academic excellence earned her a Rotary scholarship for a year of research abroad, with the choice of studying in the United States or New Zealand. Drawn to the idea of exploring a country known for its stunning landscapes and innovative agricultural research, Mary chose New Zealand. In 1991, she arrived at Massey University in Palmerston North, ready to dive into her research under the guidance of a renowned professor. By a stroke of fate, that professor was also Ranjan's PhD supervisor.

A Meeting of Minds and Hearts

Our paths crossed in the laboratories and lecture halls of Massey University, where we were both immersed in the intricate world of food science. Working under the same supervisor gave us countless opportunities to collaborate, share ideas, and discover a shared passion for discovery. What began as a professional connection soon blossomed into a deep friendship. Long conversations over lab experiments turned into coffee breaks, then dinners and movies, and eventually, a realization that we were falling in love.

By 1994, Ranjan was 31, and Mary was 28, and we knew we wanted to build a life together. Our love was a celebration of two worlds, but it also came with the beautiful complexity of blending two distinct cultures and faiths. Ranjan, raised in the Hindu tradition, and Mary, a Catholic from Ireland, embraced the challenge of honouring both heritages. Our marriage was not just one ceremony—it was a vibrant tapestry of five, each reflecting the richness of our backgrounds.

Figure 1: Five different ceremonies for our inter-faith marriage. 1- March 1994 after courthouse ceremony in Palmerston North, New Zealand, 2- March 1994 at the Hindu ceremony in Wellington, New Zealand, 3 – March 1994 catholic church ceremony in Palmerton North, New Zealand, 4- 1995 Hindu wedding ceremony in India, 5 – 1995 After catholic service in Midleton, Ireland and 6- 1995 celebration cake in Ireland

The first ceremony took place in March 1994 at the marriage registry in Palmerston North, a simple yet profound moment that legally bound us as partners. Next, we celebrated with a Hindu wedding ceremony in Wellington, New Zealand, filled with vibrant rituals, colourful attire, and the warmth of our friends. Days later, we stood in a Catholic church in Palmerston North for a blessing mass, surrounded by the quiet reverence of Mary's faith. The following year, we travelled to India for a traditional Hindu ceremony in Ranjan's hometown, where the air was filled with the scents of incense and the joy of family. Finally, in Midleton, Ireland, we completed our journey with a Catholic service, followed by a celebration complete with a towering cake, made by Mary's mum, that symbolized our shared future. Each ceremony was a chapter in our love story, a testament to our commitment to honouring both our roots and our shared dreams.

Building a Family and a Philosophy

From our union came two incredible boys, Corann and Ronan, both born in New Zealand. Raising them in a bicultural household was a joy and a learning experience, as we wove together the traditions, stories, and values of our upbringings. Our home was filled with the aromas of Indian spices one day and the comfort of Irish food the next, a reflection of the life we were building together.

Our middle-class roots shaped us in profound ways. Ranjan's childhood in a bustling household of five siblings taught him resourcefulness and the art of making do with less. Mary's upbringing in a family of four, with a stay-at-home mother and a hardworking father, instilled a similar sense of frugality and appreciation for the simple things. Neither of our families had a roadmap for financial success, but they gave us something even more valuable: a mindset of resilience and contentment.

As we navigated life as a married couple, we began to develop a financial philosophy that would become the cornerstone of our journey to independence. We called it "**Slow Spending**." It was not about deprivation or chasing wealth for its own sake; it was about intentionality, making deliberate choices about how we spent, saved, and invested our money. Slow Spending meant pausing to ask, "Do we need this? Does it align with our values?" It was about finding joy in what we had rather than always chasing more.

The Path to Financial Freedom

Our early years together were modest. As graduate students, we lived on tight budgets, stretching every dollar while pouring our energy into our research and our growing family. But even in those lean times, we began to apply the principles of **Slow Spending**. As we explain the in the next Section, **Slow Spending** refers to a combination of strategies that help in constantly spending less than the total earnings.

We cooked at home, sharing meals that blended our culinary traditions. We sought out free or low-cost activities, like visiting library, picnics at New Zealand's breathtaking parks or spending evenings with friends. Most of our furniture and household goods were purchased from so called "garage sales" in New Zealand, where people sell surplus items at throwaway prices. Initially, we saved diligently, not because we had grand ambitions of wealth, but because we wanted the freedom to live life on our terms. As Ranjan had moved from India, he was constantly converting NZ dollar to Indian Rupees and was horrified with exorbitant price upon currency conversion! It took him a while to realise that he was earning and living in New Zealand and prices in India had no bearing to the prices in New Zealand.

Over time, **Slow Spending** became more than a habit—it became a system. We prioritized experiences over possessions, invested in our education and skills, and made thoughtful decisions about our careers. Ranjan's expertise in food science led to opportunities in academia and industry, while Mary's research opened doors to industry and innovation projects. Together, we built a stable foundation, not by chasing quick wins but by consistently making choices that aligned with our long-term goals.

By our forties, we began to see the fruits of our approach. Our savings grew, and we invested in properties, focusing on low-risk, long-term strategies. We paid off our home, avoided debt, and continued to live below our means. Slow Spending did not mean we never splurged—it meant we splurged intentionally on things that brought lasting joy, like family trips or supporting causes we cared about. By our fifties, we had achieved what many dream of: financial freedom. We were not billionaires, but we were millionaires in the sense that we had enough to live comfortably, pursue our passions, and give back to our communities.

Sharing Our Story

Now, as we reflect on our journey, we are authoring a book to share the lessons we have learned. "**Slow Spending**" is not just a financial strategy—it is a way of life. It is about rejecting the pressure to keep up with others, embracing mindfulness in how you use your resources, and building wealth not for status, but for freedom. Our story, from a Himalayan village and an Irish town to a life of purpose and security, is proof that ordinary people can achieve extraordinary things with patience and intention.

We hope our tale inspires you to look at your own journey, to see the beauty in starting small, and to trust that slow, steady steps can lead to remarkable destinations. Whether you are just beginning or well on your way, the principles of Slow Spending can guide you toward a life of meaning, connection, and financial independence.

What is slow spending?

Here is our theory of what is slow spending.

Time versus Income and Spending

We have tried to develop a theory, to understand how we have been able to achieve financial success in our lives.

As we have learnt, the financial well-being is not merely a function of how much one earns—it is deeply rooted in how one chooses to spend. Two individuals with identical incomes can end up with vastly different financial outcomes depending on their spending behaviour. The relationship between **income**, **spending**, and **the time** creates fundamental patterns that determine financial outcomes over a lifetime.

To understand, the concept of "**slow spending**," we have prepared a simplified graph (Figure 2) that illustrates a critical concept in personal finance: how spending habits relative to income create distinct zones of financial stress or financial freedom that compound over time. This graph effectively visualizes this divergence over time. It captures the dynamic interplay between income and expenditure, illustrating how consistent choices either create a growing cushion of **financial freedom** or spiral into a widening gap of **financial stress**.

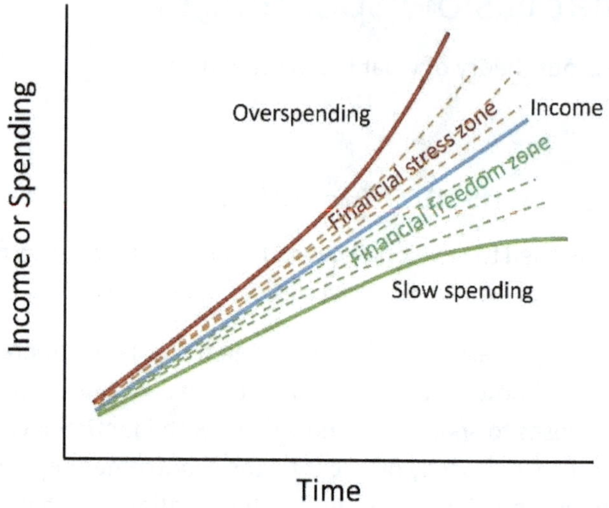

Figure 2: Spending trajectories with time. "**Slow spending**" refers to constantly reducing the rate of spending with respect to the rate of income. In a mathematical term, we are constantly reducing the slope of the "time versus spending" curve with time. "Overspending" refers to spending beyond means, where the slope of "time versus spending" curve increases with time.

So, what is "Slow Spending"?

"Slow Spending" does not imply deprivation. Rather, it reflects intentional, value-based expenditure. It involves:

- Constantly spending less than earnings and constantly and incrementally improving the saving habits (alike the Japanese term Kaizen)
- Prioritizing needs over wants.

- Avoiding impulsive purchases
- Delaying gratification to achieve larger goals
- Investing in long-term assets instead of short-term pleasures

Most of us can understand the role of slow spending but being human, we often get carried away in deviating from these principles.

Understanding the Axes and Lines

The **horizontal axis** represents **time**, moving from the beginning of our earning life (perhaps early adulthood) toward older age. The **vertical axis** represents **either income or spending** — two financial indicators that typically increase as life progresses.

There are three primary curves in the diagram:

1. **Income Line (blue)** – This line rises consistently over time. It assumes that your income increases due to promotions, experience, career shifts, or passive income sources like investments or business ownership. For simplicity, we have made this line a straight line but, in reality, it may not be a straight-line as the income may not increase linearly with time.

2. **Spending Lines (green)** – This is a more modestly increasing line, showing a restrained or "slow" increase in spending over time.

3. **Spending Lines (red)** – This is a slightly fast increasing line, showing an unrestrained or "fast" increase in spending over time.

The Financial Freedom Zone

Between these two lines — income and spending — lies the **"financial freedom zone",** the area below the income line. This area represents the difference between what you earn and what you spend. The larger this area, the more financial security you build. This gap is essentially your **savings and potential investment capital**. In our case, we have seen a widening of this area as we got older.

As illustrated by the downward arrows pointing from the income line to the slow spending line, the financial freedom zone grows larger over time if you keep spending under control. This widening gap offers you the flexibility to:

- Save consistently.
- Invest in assets that generate passive income.
- Build an emergency fund.
- Afford big-ticket items without debt.
- Eventually retire early or work less.

Why the Slope Matters

The **slope** of the green line (slow spending) is the key for understanding the curve. A steep slope would indicate fast-rising expenses — perhaps driven by lifestyle inflation, impulse purchases, or poor budgeting. But when the green line's slope is deliberately kept gentle by frugality and saving, it leads to the financial freedom. This conscious effort to lower the slope of spending curve is the essence of slow spending. You may still enjoy life and spend on what matters, but you are doing it in a way that keeps your financial headroom (the gap between income and spending) large and growing.

Over time, several things can help with financial discipline and reducing the slope of the green line:

- Increased financial literacy: You learn from experience and become more deliberate in how you manage money.
- Less peer pressure: As you age, you are less influenced by trends or status-driven spending.
- Higher earnings: With career progression, your income often increases more quickly than your basic living expenses.
- Settled lifestyle: You may have paid off debts, raised children, or downsized housing, leading to fewer big expenses.
- Stronger habits: By then, budgeting, saving, and investing may be second nature.

All these help in maintaining or even improving your spending discipline, making the financial freedom zone wider and easier to grow.

As we have mentioned before, "Slow spending" is not about deprivation — it is about intentionality. It is about aligning your spending with your values, avoiding lifestyle creep, and giving yourself the best chance at long-term financial well-being. The graph above makes it clear: the larger the gap you maintain between your income and your spending, the more financial freedom you create. And with time, that freedom compounds — just like your savings.

The "Slow Spending" Philosophy

Slow spending represents a deliberate approach to consumption that prioritizes long-term financial health over immediate gratification. It means you must build wealth with intention rather than leftovers from spendings. This concept extends beyond simple frugality—it is about creating intentional friction between income and expenditure to generate consistent surplus.

The Bigger Picture

The above figure encourages a long-term mindset. Financial independence is not about earning a huge salary overnight. It is about controlling what you do with the money you already earn and being consistent in doing so. By focusing on spending less than you earn — and keeping that gap as wide as possible — you gradually build wealth. That gap funds your savings, investments, and ultimately gives you choices in life. You could:

- Work less or retire earlier.
- Start a business.
- Help family or contribute to causes you care about
- Emergency fund development: Building resilience against unexpected expenses

- Investment capital accumulation: Creating opportunities for compound growth.
- Reduced financial anxiety: Operating with margins that buffer against income fluctuations.
- Increased optionality: Having resources available for opportunities or life changes

Financial Stress Zone

The **financial stress zone** (red zone above the income line in Figure 2) emerges when spending consistently exceeds income, creating a widening gap that becomes increasingly difficult to bridge. This zone represents more than just temporary overspending—it is a systemic pattern that accelerates financial vulnerability over time. This behaviour may reflect or bringing up or habits developed while growing up. When spending habits exceed or closely follow one's income over time, a financial stress zone emerges. This behaviour can stem from several reasons:

- Lifestyle inflation: As income increases, so do expenses. People buy more expensive homes, cars, gadgets, vacations, or luxury services.
- Lack of budgeting: Without a financial plan, spending can easily become reactive rather than intentional.
- Debt dependence: Credit cards, personal loans, and "buy now, pay later" schemes create an illusion of affordability while increasing long-term obligations.
- Keeping up with others: Social pressure and comparison often lead to unnecessary spending to match peers.
- Increases in essential spendings: such as starting family or getting education loans.

One needs to keep in mind that there is a compound effect of financial deterioration. Unlike simple arithmetic deficits, this pattern creates exponential challenges because:

- Debt accumulates with interest, making the gap between income and spending grow faster than either component alone.
- Credit utilization increases, often leading to higher interest rates and reduced borrowing capacity.
- Emergency preparedness diminishes, making individuals more vulnerable to unexpected expenses.
- Investment opportunities are foregone, missing potential compound growth.

The mathematical reality can be stark: if spending grows at a rate faster than income, the deficit does not just add up—it multiplies. A person spending $500 more than they earn monthly does not just face a $6,000 annual shortfall; they face $6,000 plus interest, plus the opportunity cost of investments not made, plus reduced financial flexibility for future income fluctuations. This is one fear that we always had in the back of our minds.

There may be several factors contribute to entering and expanding the financial stress zone. First, lifestyle inflation occurs when individuals increase their spending as their income rises, often to match societal expectations or personal desires for a higher standard of living. For example, a young professional might start with a modest car but upgrade to a luxury vehicle as their salary increases, stretching their budget beyond sustainable limits. Second, unexpected life events—

medical emergencies, job loss, or economic downturns—can exacerbate the situation, especially if there is no financial cushion. Arrival of a new baby can also be a factors. In such circumstances, a lack of financial literacy or planning, such as failing to budget or save, can lead to habitual overspending.

The consequences of residing in the Financial Stress Zone can be profound. Short-term effects include reliance on credit cards or loans, accruing interest that compounds the debt. Over time, this can lead to chronic stress, strained relationships, and even mental health challenges, as financial worries dominate daily life. The widening of this zone, as shown in the graph, suggests a feedback loop: as debt grows, individuals may work longer hours or take on additional jobs, reducing time for rest or skill development, which could otherwise increase earning potential. This cycle can trap individuals or families in a state of perpetual financial insecurity.

The financial stress zone creates psychological burdens that can perpetuate the cycle. Chronic financial stress leads to decision fatigue, reduced cognitive capacity for long-term planning, and often reactive spending patterns that worsen the situation. The stress zone becomes self-reinforcing as individuals make increasingly desperate financial decisions to maintain short-term stability.

One of the ways that we have avoided this trap is by keeping the same lifestyle that we were used to with our low income over many years. We have later in life splashed on gadgets, subscriptions and cars etc, however, that was only feasible once we knew that our spendings were not going to create new debt and we had cash to buy.

Transitioning to Slow Spending

Transitioning from the Financial Stress Zone to the Financial Freedom Zone is possible with intentional actions that you must take in your daily life.

If you would like to follow the "**slow spending**" pathways, it is never too late. However, the "**Slow Spending**" approach, leading to the "Financial Freedom Zone" (green line), requires a deliberate strategy where spending is kept below income (way below the income in as our case). **Slow Spending** requires a mindset shift. It involves prioritizing needs over wants, delaying gratification, and building a budget that accounts for both current expenses and future goals. For example, instead of dining out frequently, one might cook at home and allocate the savings to payback a loan or invest. This approach aligns with principles of financial minimalism, where the focus is on value rather than volume of consumption. Over time, as depicted in the graph, this habit creates a widening Financial Freedom Zone, where passive income from investments can eventually replace active earnings.

Several elements determine the success of Slow Spending and the expansion of the Financial Freedom Zone. First, income growth plays a role. A steady increase in earnings, whether through career progression or side hustles, provides more room to save. Second, investment strategies—such as contributing to a superannuation fund in Australia (equivalent of 401(k) in US), investing in stocks/shares, or real estate—amplify the effects of saving. Compound interest, often called the eighth wonder of the world, allows small, consistent investments to grow significantly over decades. For instance, investing $500 monthly at an average 7% return from age 30 to 60 could yield over $700,000 by retirement!

Discipline and education are also key. Understanding financial products, tax advantages, and market trends empowers individuals to make informed decisions. Additionally, life stage matters: starting Slow Spending early maximizes the time horizon for growth, while beginning later requires more aggressive saving or higher returns. The graph's gentle upward curve for the Financial Freedom Zone suggests a sustainable, gradual build-up, contrasting with the steep climb of financial stress.

Over time, these steps narrow the Financial Stress Zone and widen the Financial Freedom Zone, as illustrated in our graph.

Visual Takeaways from the Graph

The graph is more than an abstract concept. It offers practical insights:

- **Watch your slope**: Spending that increases faster than income is unsustainable.
- **Avoid the red zone**: Any time you are spending more than you earn, you're entering a danger zone—even if temporarily.
- **Aim for the green zone**: Spending less than you earn, even slightly, shifts you toward financial freedom.
- **Gaps widen over time**: The longer a behaviour continues, the greater its impact—positive or negative.

In summary, Slow spending operates on several key principles that distinguish it from restrictive budgeting:

Conscious consumption: Every purchase decision involves deliberate consideration of value, necessity, and long-term impact. This doesn't mean avoiding all discretionary spending, but rather ensuring each expenditure aligns with broader financial goals. We still own second hand furniture that we acquired free or cheap as we know that there is no end to upgrading such items in life.

Time-based decision making: Implementing waiting periods for non-essential purchases allows for more rational evaluation and often reveals that many desired items aren't needed.

Value optimization: Focusing on cost-per-use metrics rather than absolute price, leading to better long-term value even when initial costs are higher. We have found this useful while shopping for grocery items where we compare price per kg rather than the unit price.

Lifestyle design: Consciously choosing a lifestyle that provides satisfaction while requiring less financial input, often through prioritizing experiences over possessions, maintaining items longer, and finding fulfillment in non-monetary activities.

Always spending less than earnings: this is the fundamental principle of the concept. No matter how low your income becomes, you must find ways of spending less than earnings. Under such circumstances you might want to find extra work to boost your earnings.

Overall, the core principles of Slow spending are the consistent habits of financial discipline in life. With slow spending, we build that discipling over time, and it forms our financial habits that lead to secure financial freedom later in life. Slow spending is not a quick path for financial freedom, but rather a long-term commitment for spending below your means and constantly saving and investing.

How to slow spend

The overall aim of the "**slow spending**" is to constantly spend below the income line and gradually decrease the slope of the curve as shown below. The aim is to improve the area of the financial freedom zone as we get older. From our experience, we can confirm that it usually does get easier as we get older. We are assuming that the earning is increasing with time, but **what we want to focus on is the spending, saving and investment**.

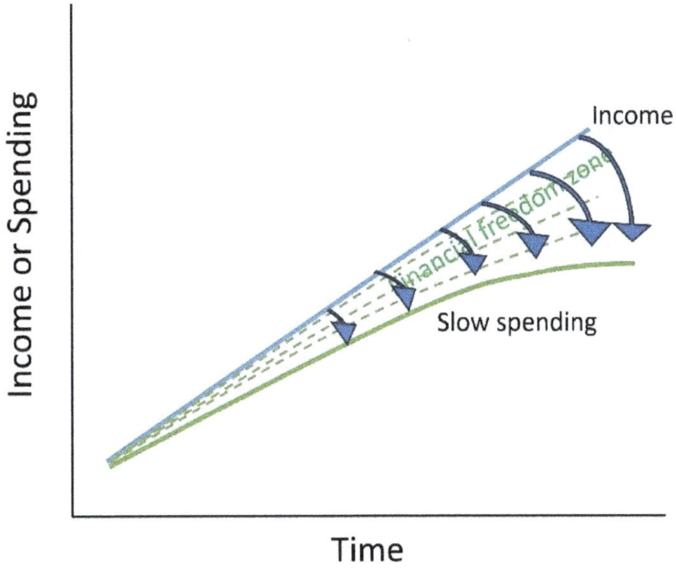

Figure 3: What really needs to happen in **Slow Spending**. Over time, the slope of spending curve needs to decrease, continuously expanding the financial freedom zone.

The above figure is a simple but powerful visual representation of how adopting a "slow spending" lifestyle can help increase our financial independence over time. In practice, implementing slow spending requires discipline and foresight. It may involve budgeting, prioritizing needs over wants, and making strategic investment choices. As the graph implies, the benefits of this approach are cumulative, with the financial freedom zone expanding most notably in the later stages of life. This visual representation serves as a motivational tool, encouraging individuals to adopt a long-term perspective on their financial habits to secure a more comfortable and independent future.

There is another way we can explain this here. Life is life a Swiss army knife and it gives you opportunities to save money in numerous ways, just like a Swiss army knife that has a range of tools that you can use depending on the task in hand. In terms of “slow spending”, the objective is to act a like a Swiss army knife where more tools you use, more valuable it becomes.

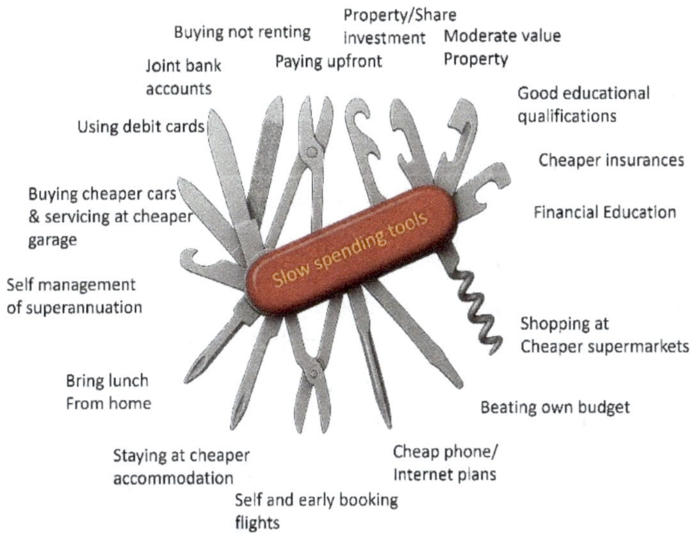

Figure 4: Slow spending tools. More you use better the financial outcome.

Life presents us with countless opportunities to manage money wisely—if we choose to recognise them. A powerful way to visualize this idea is by comparing financial discipline to a Swiss army knife. Just as a Swiss army knife offers multiple tools to handle different tasks—cutting, opening, tightening, fixing—life provides us with various "slow spending tools" that we can use depending on our needs, situations, and priorities.

As an analogy, at the centre is the red pocketknife handle labelled **"Slow spending tools"**, symbolizing the core principle of mindful and strategic spending. Extending from this handle are various "blades" or strategies—each one representing a different practical approach to reduce costs, avoid unnecessary expenses, and increase savings over time.

The idea is simple yet powerful: the more tools you actively use, the more valuable your approach becomes. Each small act may not seem significant in isolation, but together, they contribute to substantial long-term savings and financial freedom, as we have found in our lifetime.

For example, instead of relying on credit cards that often carry high interest rates, **using debit cards** ensures that you're spending only what you have. Similarly, **joint bank accounts** promote transparency and help couples or families stay on track with shared financial goals.

Buying not renting and **property/share investment** represent bigger financial decisions that can significantly boost long-term wealth. While renting offers flexibility, buying builds equity. Likewise, **investing in property or shares** rather than letting money sit idle can multiply your savings, particularly if done with patience and knowledge.

Another key habit is **paying upfront** rather than relying on payment plans or credit, which often come with hidden fees or interest. This habit not only saves money but instils financial discipline.

Choosing moderate value property, rather than stretching to buy your "dream home," is another essential slow saving principle. It leaves room for other investments and reduces long-term financial strain.

On the daily or monthly level, tools like **bringing lunch from home**, **shopping at cheaper supermarkets**, and **buying cheaper cars and servicing them at affordable garages** offer consistent savings. These are classic examples of lifestyle choices that align with the slow spending philosophy—saving small amounts regularly rather than chasing big, rare windfalls.

Staying at cheaper accommodation when traveling or living and **booking flights early** are also practical tools. These do not compromise the experience, but they do cut costs significantly with just a little forethought.

In today's digital age, opting for **cheap phone and internet plans** can save hundreds annually. Many people overpay for services they barely use—being mindful about these costs can be an easy win.

More technical yet vital tools include **self-management of superannuation** (or retirement funds), which we found has led us to better returns and reduced fees. Likewise, **financial education** and **good educational qualifications** are foundational investments. They may not produce immediate savings but equip you with knowledge and skills that pay dividends over a lifetime—either through better career opportunities or smarter money decisions.

Cheaper insurances—health, car, home—also fall under this philosophy. Rather than blindly renewing existing policies, comparing options and negotiating better deals can save substantial amounts.

Importantly, **beating your own budget** is not about deprivation—it is a challenge to spend less than you plan to, not out of fear, but for future gains.

Each one of these strategies is a blade in your financial Swiss army knife. You do not need to use all of them at once, but the more you adopt and integrate into your life, the stronger your financial resilience becomes. Over time, these habits compound into savings, security, and eventually, **financial freedom**.

Slow spending, then, is not about cutting out joy or living without comfort—it is about choosing smarter paths that align with long-term goals. Like a Swiss army knife, life hands you a set of tools. As we have learnt, the task is to use them wisely.

Early sacrifices – the pathway to financial freedom

Although our financial journey started late in life, we believe, the concept of **Slow Spending** starts early in the career life and forms the basis of financial freedom. We have tried to capture a fundamental truth in personal finance: **the quality of our financial decisions early in life profoundly shapes our financial well-being in later years**. See the Figure below. The idea of the diagram is to captures a fundamental principle in personal finance and decision-making: the trade-offs between short-term ease and long-term consequences. This message, though simple in essence, holds deep implications. The image contrasts two life trajectories—one where easy choices lead to hardship later in life, and another where disciplined choices lead to abundance later in life.

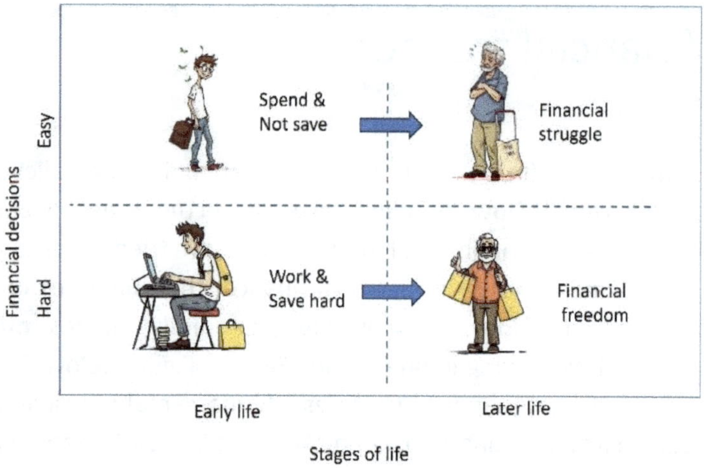

Figure 5: Financial impact of choices made in the early stage of the life.

Understanding the Core Principle: Easy Now, Hard Later vs. Hard Now, Easy Later

At the heart of above illustration is a powerful idea: **delayed gratification**. In the top half of the diagram, we see a young person who chooses to enjoy life immediately spending freely, perhaps living beyond their means, and postponing the difficult conversations around budgeting, investing, or saving. The result, as shown, is an older person grappling with **financial stress**, a product of years of unplanned spending and lack of financial discipline.

In contrast, the bottom half of the diagram features a young individual working hard, sacrificing luxuries, and diligently saving. This path involves making tough decisions early—

perhaps foregoing vacations, resisting peer pressure, and choosing long-term security over short-term pleasure. But the payoff is immense: financial freedom in later years, symbolized by the confident and content older individual who now enjoys life without the constant worry of money.

This stark contrast encapsulates a widely accepted principle in behavioural finance: **humans are naturally inclined toward short-term rewards**, even when this undermines their long-term well-being. Overcoming this instinct is the cornerstone of smart financial planning.

In conclusion, our conceptual diagram (Figure 3) uses just four images and two arrows to tell a story that affects every human being. It reminds us that **every financial decision is a brick in the foundation of our future.** At the heart of the diagram is the concept of delayed gratification, a psychological principle that plays a pivotal role in financial success. We believe a fundamental understanding of this graph is an integral part of building wealth through slow spending.

How we became millionaires by slow spending

As we have discussed in the Introduction Chapter, we come from middle classes with humble beginnings. When we finished our studies, and got married, we were 31 and 28 with less than A$10,000 in total savings. Our financial journey began with good educational qualification, financial education, and property investments. Along the way we raised two kids and worked in 3 countries: New Zealand, Denmark, and Australia.

As we reflect on your life pathways, we have pulled out the steps that we think that have helped us become millionaires. Many of the pathways are common to everyone in a middle class no matter which part of the world you live in.

We detail some of this information as we discuss our journey in education and property investments.

Good Education

When people talk about building wealth, they often jump straight to investments or saving tips — but for us, the real foundation began with something much simpler: education.

Technical education

Both of us studied food science — Ranjan in India and New Zealand, and Mary in Ireland — and looking back, that decision has paid off in more ways than we could have imagined. Choosing to pursue higher education in a practical, science-based field set the foundation for not only a fulfilling career but also a stable and secure financial future.

Food science is one of those disciplines that will always remain relevant. Regardless of how the world changes, people will always need safe, nutritious, and enjoyable food. That meant we were entering an industry that is relatively stable and consistently in demand. The technical knowledge we gained — in food safety, processing, nutrition, and product development — gave us a strong edge in the job market. And more than just helping us find employment, our degrees helped us land meaningful, well-paying roles early in our careers.

Figure 6: Mary and Ranjan are indebted to two institutions for their technical education: University college Cork, Ireland and Massey University, New Zealand, respectively

But good education does not just provide technical knowledge; it opens doors. For both of us, education was the first step in building long-term careers. Over time, we were able to specialize, take on leadership roles, and move into areas that aligned with our interests and values. As our responsibilities grew, so did our incomes. That steady increase in earnings became one of the most important pillars of our financial journey.

From the beginning, having stable jobs allowed us to make smart financial choices. We could start saving early, invest in property, and make regular contributions to our superannuation fund. We had the confidence to plan for the long term because we were not constantly stressed about making ends meet. Our education played a significant role in giving us that peace of mind.

It also gave us the freedom to say "yes" to experiences — whether that meant buying our first home, traveling as a family, or supporting our children's education. None of these decisions would have felt possible if we did not have a strong, consistent income to rely on. And that income was directly linked to the qualifications and expertise we had developed through our studies.

Good education is more than a piece of paper — it is an investment that keeps paying dividends throughout life. It sets the tone for your career, it builds your confidence, and most importantly, it empowers you to make choices with your money, your time, and your future. For us, studying food science was the beginning of a journey not just toward professional success but also toward financial freedom.

When we look back at our decision to study food science — Ranjan in India and New Zealand, and Mary in Ireland, it is clear that it shaped not just our careers but our entire financial future. A technical degree like food science may not always sound glamorous, but it is practical, versatile, and deeply tied to real-world needs. Over 30 years, that one choice has helped us build fulfilling careers, stay financially secure, and ultimately work toward financial freedom.

Why Technical Degrees Matter Financially

When students finish high school, they are often unsure which path to take: a general arts degree, a pure science stream, or a technical field such as engineering, food science, IT, or nursing. While all education has value, not all degrees offer the same return on investment. And when you look at the lifetime earnings of someone with a practical, technical qualification versus someone with a general degree, the difference is often staggering.

Let's look at the numbers. Suppose a general arts or science graduate starts with a salary of around AUD $55,000 per year and reaches around $80,000–$90,000 by mid-career. In contrast, a food science graduate may start closer to AUD $65,000–$70,000 and can easily cross $100,000–$120,000 or more within 10–15 years, especially if they move into leadership or specialist roles like quality assurance managers, product development leads, or regulatory affairs experts.

Even conservatively, that is a difference of $20,000–$30,000 per year once you're established. Over a 30-year career, that difference can add up to $600,000 to $900,000 or more — and that is without considering promotions, bonuses, or investment potential from higher savings. That is nearly a million dollars in extra income, just from choosing a technical degree wisely.

Steady Jobs Lead to Smart Financial Moves

One of the biggest advantages of having a steady, reliable job — which our food science education gave us — is the ability to plan for the long term. We were not living from pay-check to pay-check. We could set up automatic savings, build an emergency fund, invest in real estate, and contribute regularly to our superannuation (retirement) accounts.

The earlier you start, the more you benefit from the power of compounding. Because we did not delay our careers figuring out "what next," we had a financial head start. Over 25+ years, that steady income and smart investing have added up to significant wealth.

It is not just about the money either. A secure job gave us peace of mind. We could make decisions like taking family holidays, helping relatives, or funding our children's education without constant financial pressure. That freedom came from choosing a field where employment is steady, well-paid, and respected.

Education is often described as the key to opportunity. But for us, it was more than that — it was a launchpad. It gave us confidence, skills, and financial independence. When you choose the right field, a degree is not just a qualification; it is a tool for building the life you want.

Final Thoughts: Choosing Wisely Pays Off

To those considering their future — or guiding their children through career decisions — our advice is simple: choose a degree that leads somewhere. Arts and general science degrees have their place, especially when paired with other qualifications. But if you are looking for job security, consistent income, and long-term financial success, a technical, engineering or applied science degree like food science can be one of the smartest moves you ever make.

Over 30 years, that choice has easily made a **million-dollar** difference in our household. And just as importantly, it gave us the confidence to dream, plan, and live life on our terms. Education is not just about what you learn — it is about what that learning allows you to do.

Master of Business Administration (MBA)

To support and complement our professional careers, we both decided to pursue a Master of Business Administration (MBA) from reputable Australian universities. An MBA is a postgraduate degree that focuses on developing skills in leadership, strategic thinking, finance, marketing, and general management. Unlike technical or subject-specific degrees, an MBA is designed to equip professionals with a broader understanding of how businesses operate and grow. It's especially valuable for those seeking to move into leadership roles, start their own business, or simply develop a well-rounded perspective on financial and organizational decision-making.

Pursuing an MBA was no easy task. We both completed our degrees part-time while continuing to work full-time in our careers in food science. This meant long evenings, weekends filled with assignments, and juggling the demands of work, study, and family life. We did not study at the same time—rather, we staggered our degrees so we could support one another and the family during the most intense periods of study. While it was a tough few years, it was one of the most rewarding investments we made in ourselves.

For Ranjan, the MBA was instrumental in providing the knowledge and confidence needed to start his own business. With a strong background in food science and industry experience, he had the technical side well covered. But managing a business requires more than just technical knowledge—it involves budgeting, forecasting, pricing, marketing, and understanding the broader financial health of the business. The MBA helped fill those knowledge gaps. Concepts such as cash flow management, cost structures, business planning, and strategic positioning became critical tools that Ranjan applied when setting up and running his company.

For Mary, the MBA opened doors to senior management positions in the corporate world. It allowed her to move beyond the technical aspects of her role and demonstrate her ability to lead teams, manage budgets, and contribute to strategic decision-making at the executive level. This career progression had a direct and positive impact on our household income and long-term financial stability. The MBA gave her the skills and credentials needed to step into leadership roles, and the confidence to speak the language of business in boardrooms and management meetings.

Beyond the immediate career benefits, both of us found that the MBA improved our financial literacy—something that played a crucial role in our journey toward financial independence. We became more comfortable reading balance sheets, understanding investment risks, and making informed decisions about our personal finances. The critical thinking and analytical skills we developed through the MBA helped us assess opportunities more clearly and avoid common financial mistakes.

In hindsight, completing our MBAs was one of the smartest financial decisions we made. While the upfront cost—both time and money—was significant, the long-term returns have been well worth it. It was not just a qualification; it was a mindset shift that empowered us to think bigger, plan better, and take control of our financial future.

But of course, income alone does not build wealth. What really helped was combining that solid income with **slow and mindful spending**. We have always been conscious of how we spend money — not in a stingy way, but in a way that reflects our values. We did not try to keep up with trends or compare ourselves to others. Instead, we focused on what was really important to us, and that has made an enormous difference.

Looking back, investing in our education was one of the best financial decisions we ever made. It gave us confidence, stability, and options. And when paired with conscious spending, it became a powerful formula for building long-term wealth and peace of mind. In fact, we think of our financial approach like this: education gave us the engine, but **slow spending** kept the car running smoothly without breaking down.

Gaining financial education

When we first started our journey, we did not come from a business or finance background. We had no training in economics or money management. Like many people, we had to learn things from scratch. What we did have, though, was a strong desire to understand how to make the most of our hard-earned money. Over time, this curiosity helped us build confidence, and more importantly, it helped us make practical financial decisions that worked for us. As we mentioned above, along our career pathways, we both gained MBA degrees by part-time studying, so that significantly contributed towards foundations of our financial education.

We knew from early on that if we wanted to build a secure financial future, we had to educate ourselves. No one was going to do it for us. We read a lot—mostly free resources online and magazines available in Australia. One magazine, called *Money Magazine*, became one of our key tools for which initially we had paid subscription. It helped break down complicated financial concepts into everyday language. It covered things like budgeting, superannuation, investment options, insurance, and tips on getting out of debt. Slowly, issue by issue, we started making sense of how money works. We also started using online resources. Online resources were also very helpful. There are many websites and blogs that explain financial topics in simple terms. We found that reading articles and watching videos made it easier to grasp innovative ideas. Websites like the Australian Securities and Investments Commission (ASIC) and Money Smart (https://moneysmart.gov.au/) provided free guides on budgeting and investing.

We did not try to become experts overnight. Instead, we focused on making small changes and better decisions. The magazine helped us understand consumer finance and how small savings here and there could grow into bigger savings over time. One article might explain how to save on groceries, while another would talk about the benefits of paying off your mortgage early. We took notes, talked about what we learned, and tried to apply the tips in our everyday life.

When it came to investing, we decided to keep things simple. We did not want to take big risks. We understood that some people made big profits through high-risk ventures like cryptocurrency, art, or collectibles, but we did not feel comfortable going down that road. Our personalities just did not match that kind of high-stakes game. Instead, we stuck to the basics.

For us, "bricks and mortar" — that is, property — felt safe and understandable. There was something solid about owning a piece of land or a house. It is a physical thing you can see and touch. You do not need to be an expert to know that people will always need a place to live, and if you buy wisely, property generally holds its value or even increases over time.

So, over the years, we made most of our investments in property. Sometimes we lived in the homes ourselves, and at other times we rented them out. We learned about the importance of location, upkeep, and rental yields. It was not always smooth — there were repairs, tenant issues, and rising interest rates to deal with — but overall, property gave us peace of mind.

Even though we played it safe, we did not completely ignore other investment options. Eventually, we started learning about the share market. We did not jump in straight away, though. First, we read about it. We tried to understand what shares really were — how companies work, what dividends are, and why share prices go up and down.

Again, we kept it simple. We did not try to chase the latest "hot stock." Instead, we looked at long-term investing. We preferred well-established companies that paid steady dividends and had a good track record. We were happy with slow and steady growth. We also considered index funds, which spread your money across many companies, reducing the risk of relying on just one.

The more we read, the more we understood our own risk profile. Some people are naturally drawn to high-risk, high-reward options. That is not us. We have always preferred the idea of protecting what we have rather than gambling for more. We were gradually building up our assets. That is why we have never touched things like cryptocurrency. We know people who have made money with it, but we also know people who lost thousands when the market crashed. That is not a rollercoaster we want to ride.

We always focused on what we understood: saving regularly, living significantly below our means (**slow spending**), and maximising the paying off investment property loans. As we elaborate in the property investment section, we were frantically paying off property loans no matter which property we had.

Financial education helped us keep track of our spending, avoided unnecessary debt, and made sure we had insurance in place to protect our family and property. One important thing we have learned is that financial success is not about luck or getting in early on a hot trend. It is about steady habits, discipline, and patience. We tried to make our money work for us without losing sleep at night. That is why we preferred investments that did not need constant monitoring or cause stress.

Today, when we look back, we feel proud of the choices we made. It was not always easy, and we made our share of mistakes (for example, we had some bad property investments), but we learned from them. Our slow and cautious approach allowed us to pay off the properties, create a comfortable lifestyle, and prepare for the future.

We are still learning. The world of finance keeps changing, and new opportunities pop up all the time. But we stay grounded in what works for us. We read, we discuss, and we keep improving.

If there is one piece of advice, we could give others in the same boat — people without a business or finance background — it would be this: Do not be afraid to learn. Start small. Read simple, reliable sources. Talk to others. Ask questions. And do not feel pressured to take big risks just because someone else is doing it.

We have always had a low risk profile when it comes to investing. This means we prefer investments that are less likely to lose value, even if they do not offer the highest returns. We knew that higher returns usually come with higher risk, and we were not comfortable taking big chances with our hard-earned money.

Although we were heavily concentrated on property investments, later in life we also learned about the importance of diversification. This means not putting all our eggs in one basket. Even though we invested mostly in property, we made sure to have some savings in the bank (e.g. term deposits) and maximised contribution to our superannuation (the Australian version of a retirement fund). This way, if one investment did not do well, we would not lose everything. Maximising superannuation contributions is one of the safest and most profitable investments in our future.

Looking back, we realize how important it is to educate yourself about money. Even if you do not have a background in business or finance, there are many resources available to help you learn. Magazines like "Money Magazine" and online articles can make complex topics easier to understand.

We also learned that it is okay to take things slowly. You do not have to rush into making big investment decisions. It is better to take your time, do your research, and make choices that you feel comfortable with.

You do not need a degree in finance to make smart money choices. All you need is a willingness to learn, some patience, and the courage to make thoughtful decisions. If we could do it, so can you.

Our Advice to Others

If you are just starting out with saving and investing, here are a few tips based on our experience:

- **Start with the basics:** Learn about budgeting, saving, and the different types of investments.
- **Use trusted resources:** Magazines, books, and reputable websites can help you understand financial concepts.
- **Keep it simple:** Do not feel pressured to invest in things you do not understand. Start with low-risk options like property or shares in well-known companies.
- **Diversify:** Do not put all your money in one place. Spread your investments to reduce risk.
- **Be patient:** Investing is a long-term game. Do not panic if the market goes down; focus on your goals.
- **Avoid high-risk assets unless you are confident:** Only invest in things like cryptocurrency or collectibles if you fully understand the risks.

Conclusions

Our journey in saving and investing has been and will be a learning experience. By starting with the basics, using trusted resources like "Money Magazine," and keeping our investments simple, we have been able to grow our wealth without taking on too much risk. We have learned that it is okay to take things slowly and that financial education is an ongoing process. Most importantly, we have realized that you do not need to be an expert to make smart financial decisions – you just need to be willing to learn and take things one step at a time.

Throughout our journey, we have stayed true to our low-risk philosophy. We have never been tempted by get-rich-quick schemes or flashy investment trends. Our focus has always been on building wealth gradually, mainly through property investment, without stress or sleepless nights. We have made mistakes along the way, like underestimating maintenance costs for our investment property or hesitating too long before entering the share market. But each mistake was a chance to learn and refine our approach.

Looking back, we are proud of how far we have come. From knowing almost nothing about finance, we have built a solid foundation for our future. *Money Magazine* and online resources gave us the tools to understand consumer finance, while our cautious mindset kept us grounded. We are not financial experts, and we do not need to be. By keeping things simple, staying informed, and sticking to low-risk investments like property and shares, we have created a financial plan that works for us.

We have realised that the science and financial education were two key pillars of our "Slow Spending" philosophy to get rich.

Staying together as a couple

In a world where relationships often feel fragile, it might seem old-fashioned to talk about marriage as a powerful tool for financial success and personal growth. However, after over 30 years of marriage, we firmly believe that love and money truly can go hand-in-hand, and staying married can be one of the smartest long-term financial decisions we have ever made.

Our journey has not always been easy. Like many couples, we faced arguments, misunderstandings, and tough times, especially concerning money – deciding how to manage our finances, what to spend, how much to save, and how to invest. Then came the challenges of raising two children, juggling responsibilities, and navigating each other's emotional difficulties. When we moved to Denmark, we also had to travel and juggle two jobs and two little kids. Yet, we made a conscious choice to stay together and work through these issues. Over time, we not only grew stronger emotionally but also became incredibly stronger financially. Looking back, sticking together was one of the smartest financial decisions of our lives. This stability allowed us to consistently apply our "slow spending" approach, which we believe is key to building lasting wealth.

The Hidden Costs of Separation: Why Divorce Drains Your Wallet

One of the most compelling reasons to build a lasting marriage is to avoid the immense financial burden of divorce. Divorce rates are significant; for example, in the US, about 39% of first marriages end in divorce, with numbers rising for subsequent marriages. The CDC's National Center for Health Statistics reported around 689,000 divorces in the U.S. alone in 2021. In Australia, around 33% of marriages end in divorce, with an average length of around 12 years before separation. While separation is sometimes necessary, especially in cases of abuse or trauma, many couples split over issues that could potentially be resolved, particularly financial disagreements.

The financial toll of divorce is devastating. When you separate, you are not just dividing your possessions; you are often **doubling your living expenses**. Imagine paying for two rents or mortgages, two sets of utility bills, and two grocery budgets – it adds up incredibly fast. The combined income that once comfortably covered a single household is suddenly stretched across two. Under these circumstances it becomes harder to the strategy of **Slow Spending**. This financial strain can be particularly difficult given that many people already struggle; a 2023 survey by Finder found that around 61% of Australians live pay check to pay check, with one in three having less than **$1,000 AUD in savings**. For us, it never occurred that we should stay apart. We always considered ourselves as a single unit. A strong relationship with shared goals, honest communication, and mutual support can make an enormous difference in navigating these financial realities.

Studies confirm financial devastation caused by separation. Research by AMP and the University of Canberra showed that divorced Australians are more likely to experience financial stress. Divorced women, on average, face a staggering 37% drop in their income, while divorced men face a 22% drop. This is because two households are simply more expensive than one. Beyond the everyday living costs, there are also substantial legal fees. In Australia, divorce costs can range from **$5,000 AUD to $100,000 AUD**, depending on the complexity of the case. These expenses severely hinder any "**slow spending**" strategy, diverting money away from savings and investments towards unavoidable separation costs.

A Stable Home, A Brighter Future: How Marriage Benefits Your Children

The benefits of staying together have extended far beyond just your finances and into the well-being of our children. Numerous studies highlight the positive impact of stable, two-parent households on children. Children in intact families are more likely to perform well at school, have higher self-esteem, and experience fewer behavioural problems. From a financial standpoint, raising children in one home is also significantly more efficient. We avoided buying duplicate school supplies, organising two birthday parties, or maintaining two wardrobes for alternating households. This efficiency allowed us to **direct more resources towards their education, extracurricular activities, and future savings**. Research further supports this. A 2019 report from the Institute for Family Studies revealed that children raised by married parents are significantly less likely to experience poverty – only 11% compared to 44% for children of single parents. They are also more likely to perform better academically and emotionally. Our own adult children have expressed how much it meant to them to see us work through our differences, teaching them resilience, compromise, and the true value of commitment. This stability is invaluable for a family's long-term financial security and the successful implementation of a "slow spending" lifestyle.

The "Slow Spending" Advantage: Building Wealth Together

The **"slow spending"** strategy has been a cornerstone of our financial success. This approach isn't about being miserly or denying yourselves enjoyment; instead, it means **spending mindfully, intentionally, and always below your income level**. It involves being conscious of what truly matters and cutting back on unnecessary expenses.

Staying together has allowed us to apply this strategy more effectively. By pooling incomes and dramatically cutting costs, we have been able to free up significant funds for savings and investments. For instance, the Bureau of Labor Statistics' 2022 Consumer Expenditure Survey shows that while an average single person spends about **$48,000 AUD** a year, a two-person household spends around **$70,000 AUD**. This is not double the cost, because you are sharing major expenses like rent or a mortgage, utilities, internet, and even subscriptions like Netflix. So, on average, **we have been able save $26,000 per year by living as a single-family unit**. Although we have not specifically measured this, over 30 year**, this saving becomes, a whopping $780,000**. This also means that there was more money available for us towards savings, children education and property investments, which we discuss later in this book.

Beyond Money: The Deeper Rewards of Lasting Love

While the financial benefits are substantial, staying together has also deepened our love in unexpected ways. As we have grown older, we have become closer, not just as partners but as best friends. There is something truly special about sharing decades of memories – raising children, surviving tough times, and celebrating the good ones. A 2020 study in the Journal of Social and Personal Relationships found that couples who navigate challenges together often report higher relationship satisfaction over time. For us, every hurdle we have overcome has made our bond stronger.

This is not about promoting a perfect, glamorous, or always romantic ideal of marriage. It is about a real love, built on trust and shared effort, which can lead to something incredible: a content home, a secure financial future, and a deep sense of contentment that money simply cannot buy. Through thick and thin, we discovered not just each other, but the peace, freedom, and quiet joy that comes from building a life together. This emotional payoff creates the stable foundation needed for disciplined "slow spending" and long-term financial security.

Ultimately, staying together is not just about love; it is a powerful force for financial and emotional strength. By pooling incomes, significantly reducing costs, and working through challenges as a team, we have built a life that is not only financially secure but also deeply fulfilling. Our children are thriving, our love has deepened, and our bank account is looking happier. This foundation of a strong, lasting marriage provides the stability and shared purpose needed to successfully implement "slow spending" and achieve your goal of becoming a millionaire.

Having joint bank accounts

When we got married back in 1994, it just felt natural to combine everything – our dreams, our homes, our challenges and yes, our money too. Honestly, at that time, we did not even think about keeping separate bank accounts. It was not something people around us talked about, and it certainly did not seem necessary. So, we opened one joint account, and that is how it has stayed ever since.

Now, more than 30 years later, we can confidently say that having a joint account has helped us tremendously – not just financially, but also in how we communicate, plan, and live our life as a team. We are not saying it is the only way to do things, but for us, it worked beautifully. Here is why.

Joint Bank Accounts: Why Sticking Together for 30+ Years Pays Off

When we got married in the early '90s, the idea of having separate bank accounts just did not cross our minds. In fact, at the time, we had not even heard much about couples combining their accounts—most people we knew just did what felt natural, and for us, that meant sharing everything, including our money. Looking back now, after more than three decades of marriage, we realize how much this simple decision has benefitted us in ways we did not even realize at the time.

One Account, One Fee: Keeping It Simple

Let us start with the obvious – bank fees. When you have separate accounts, you are often paying double: two monthly account-keeping fees, two sets of charges for ATM usage, two cards to maintain, and so on. Over time, this adds up.

Back in the day, banks used to charge $5 or $6 a month just for the "privilege" of holding your money. It may not sound like much, but if you are both paying that, it is $10 or $12 a month – or $120 to $150 a year – just going to the bank for doing, well, not much. Multiply that by 30 years, and you are looking at several thousand dollars just in fees that could've been avoided.

With a joint account, it's simple: one account, one fee (if any), and that is it. These days many banks do not charge anything if you meet minimum deposit conditions – and when both of your incomes flow into the same account, that is an easy box to tick.

Transparency That Builds Trust

With a joint account, every transaction is out in the open. Both partners can see what is coming in and what is going out, which means there's no hiding spending habits or financial surprises. This transparency builds trust and helps avoid misunderstandings about where the money is going. Over the years, this openness has probably saved us from countless arguments about money, because we both know exactly what is happening with our finances.

Easier Bill Paying and Budgeting

Paying bills from a joint account is a breeze. There is no need to figure out who owes what or to transfer money back and forth between accounts. Everything comes out of one place, which makes budgeting and managing household expenses much more straightforward. Over the years, this has saved us a lot of time and hassle, especially as our lives got busier with kids, jobs, and all the other things that come with adulthood.

Pooling Funds for Big Dreams

The real magic of a joint account is the ability to pool your money. When you are both tossing your pay checks into one pot, you have serious financial firepower. Early in our marriage, this let us save up faster for big goals—like the down payment on our first house. If we had kept separate accounts, it would have taken longer to scrape together that cash.

Over the decades, pooling funds has helped us crush it on so many fronts. We have renovated our home, sent kids to college, and even started a small side business, all because we could combine our resources. It is like having a superpower: two incomes, one goal. Whether it is tackling debt, building an emergency fund, or splurging on a dream vacation, a joint account makes it easier to hit those targets. Pooling also means you are both invested in the same financial future. There is no "my money" or "your money"—it is *our* money. That mindset has kept us aligned, even when we had different priorities. Maybe one of us wanted to save for a new car while the other was eyeing a kitchen upgrade. With a joint account, we would talk it out, compromise, and make it work. That teamwork has been the backbone of our financial success.

A Shared Financial Journey

There is something special about building a life with one account. Every deposit, every withdrawal, every milestone—it is a story you write together. Looking back, our bank statements are like a scrapbook of our marriage. There is the big deposit from selling our first car, the monthly payments for our daughter's braces, the random late-night pizza orders. It is not just numbers; it is *us*.

This shared journey has made us stronger as a couple. We have celebrated wins, like paying off the mortgage, and weathered losses, like unexpected car repairs. Through it all, the joint account has been our financial glue, keeping us connected and committed to each other's dreams.

Why It has Worked for 30+ Years

So, why has a joint account has worked so well for us? We believe, it is not just about the money—it is about the mindset. Combining our finances forced us to talk openly, plan together, and trust each other completely. It has turned money from a potential stressor into a tool for building our life.

Over three decades, we have seen friends struggle with separate accounts, bickering over who owes what or hiding purchases. Meanwhile, our joint account has kept things simple, transparent, and united. It has saved us cash, time, and countless arguments. More than that, it has given us the freedom to dream big and chase those dreams as a team.

Of course, having a joint account does not mean we never had disagreements. We have had our fair share of arguments about spending priorities and savings strategies. But because we shared the same account, those disagreements pushed us to talk more, understand each other's perspectives, and find a middle ground.

And over time, it became second nature. We developed shared values around money. We became aligned in how we approached both small purchases and big decisions.

Final Thoughts

For us, a joint account wasn't just about banking. It was about building a shared life, financially and emotionally. It gave us clarity, efficiency, and a sense of partnership that made us stronger as a couple. Sure, it might not work for everyone. But if both people are willing to be open and work together, a joint bank account can be a fantastic tool for growing together – not just as a couple, but as a financial team.

Looking back, we are grateful we made that choice back in 1994. It is one of the simplest decisions we ever made – and one of the best.

Here is how our joint bank accounts are structured:

Below is a simplified structure of our joint bank accounts. We started mainly using one bank (Bank A) and had a couple of accounts with them. We always made sure that none of our accounts had any annual account keeping fees. There was an everyday banking account which was linked to our credit cards for everyday spending. Everyday account earned little or no

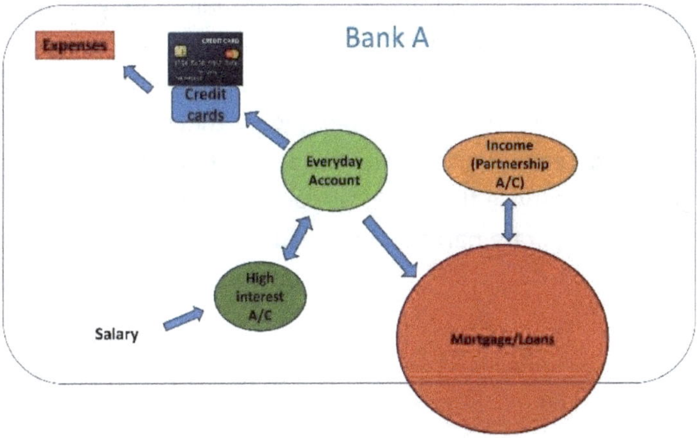

Our bank accounts – prior to 2010

bank interest. Linked to the everyday account was a high intertest account that required minimum deposit of $2000 (at the time account was opened) to have an interest. The salary would go into the high interest account. The main advantage for us having a high interest account was that this account was not accessible through our credit cards or available for day-to-day tractions, meaning that it was protected from scammers. All tractions were operated through the everyday account which was used as transit account for repayment of property investment loans and everyday spending through the credit card.

This how our tractions happened. Every time salary is received into the high interest account, most income will be transferred via everyday account to property loans. Every month, we would keep $3000-4000 as an emergency fund and less than $2000 in our everyday account. At the end of the month, any surplus money would go the property loan repayment. For running our property investments, we set up a separate business partnership structure, and all rental income were transferred to service the property loans that we had. This way the loan repayments would be far higher than what was needed to service the loans. Our accountant also appreciated having a separate partnership account for investments.

In 2010, we cancelled credit cards and switched to Debit Cards only. We have discussed the reason for this in next Section of this book. Basically, to further discipline our spending habits,

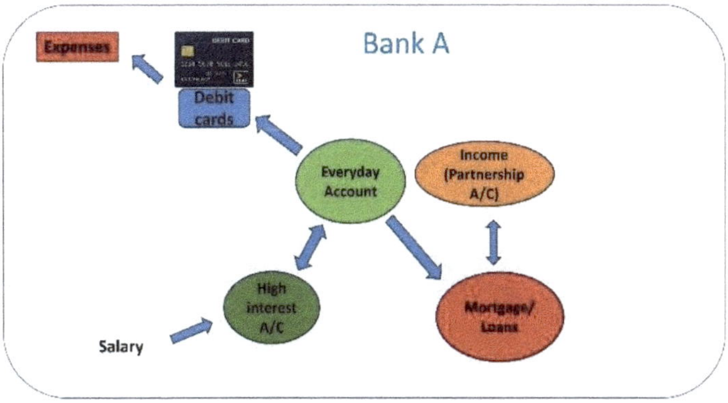

2010 – Switch from Credit to Debit cards

we decided that we will only spend what we could afford from the existing funds rather than spending through a credit card and then working out how we were going to pay for that. As we had significant efforts in repaying the property loans, our total loans were shrinking fast.

Here is the current banking structure. The main source of income remains Mary's salary. With Ranjan drawing small income from his business We have no debts, and all our accounts are generating income. We have also started a social enterprise in India with aim of helping poor women and children in training and enabling them to become entrepreneurial and self-sufficient. This project has been one of the main expenses for us for few years.

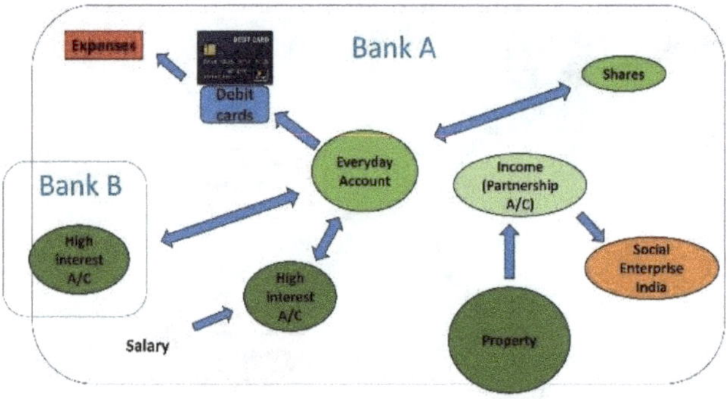

Current – Income and investment Structure

Once Mary decides to leave active employment, we aim to operate the accounts a follows. The salary will be replaced with income from our rental income and the drawings from our superannuation account. Although, the overall income will

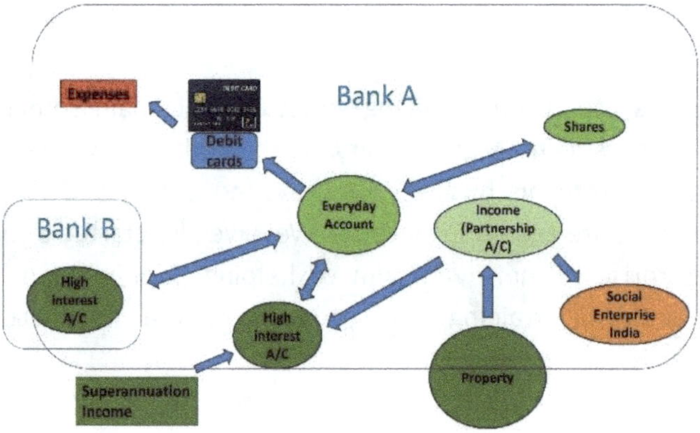

Retirement – Income and investment Structure

be lower than what the salary brings, the income will be sufficient for our needs and wants, which may include new vehicles, social enterprise in India, global travels and spending time with friends and family. Our expenses may include supporting our children in getting into their own homes.

Making harder to access our own money

One of the tricks that we have found has worked for us is keeping most of the money at an arm's length. The main reason for this is to avoid temptation of spending the extra money. Here are a couple of examples that we have used.

- Having the extra money paid into the mortgage account than keeping the extra money in off-set account. In Australia, one can link an offset account to the mortgage account which reduces the interest by the amount available in the offset account. Although it is a great strategy, a temptation remains to spend the money. However, if you have put the spare money into the mortgage account, although that money is available for discretionary spending, it usually takes a day or two to get that money into your spending account thereby removing the temptation to immediately spend it.
- Putting extra money in fixed deposit – that way there is no immediate access to the extra money.

Do away with credit cards and use only debit cards

In the world of modern finance, plastic cards dominate our wallets. Among them, two primary options stand out: credit cards and debit cards. While both provide cashless convenience, they represent fundamentally different approaches to money management. Until 2010, we did have joint credit cards, and we maximise the benefit rewards offered by these cards, however, it was

handwork to keep up with various reward programs. Most of our rewards went towards supermarket vouchers which we used for grocery shopping. Although, the credit cards worked fine for us, we decided to do away with credit cards and focus on spending on what we had and totally switched to debit cards. Although credit cards are wonderful for accumulation of travel and other rewards, they do encourage you to spend more than you wish to spend.

For individuals who value financial discipline, control over spending, and long-term financial stability, choosing a debit card over a credit card is more than just a preference—it's a strategic decision. We, like many financially mindful individuals, opted to use debit cards instead of credit cards for our daily expenses. While credit cards may offer attractive rewards and perks, we believe that the potential risks—particularly the ease of overspending and the accumulation of debt—often outweigh the benefits for the average consumer. Over the long term, this decision has led us to substantial financial security, lower stress, and greater freedom.

As the debit cards are directly linked to our bank account, meaning we can only spend the funds that we have. This simple mechanism is a powerful safeguard against the temptation to live beyond your means—a common issue with credit cards, which allow users to borrow against future income and potentially rack up high-interest debt if balances are not paid in full each month. Over two decades, consistently spending only what you have helps develop strong financial discipline, avoids debt cycles, and ensures your lifestyle aligns with your actual resources.

The Psychology of Spending: Credit vs Debit

One of the main reasons for our preference is rooted in behavioural psychology. Multiple studies have shown that people tend to spend more when using credit cards compared to cash or debit cards. When you use a credit card, you are not immediately parting with your money. This "buy now, pay later" model disconnects the act of spending from the consequence of payment.

In contrast, debit cards are tied directly to your bank account. Every transaction reflects instantly, which keeps you grounded in the reality of your current financial situation. This real-time awareness helps reinforce budgeting discipline and curtails impulse spending.

A landmark study by Prelec and Simester (2001) (*Always Leave Home Without It: A Further Investigation of the Credit-Card Effect on Willingness to Pay*. Marketing Letters, 12(1), 5-12) found that people were willing to spend up to 100% more when using credit cards compared to cash or debit. The psychological "pain of paying" is delayed with credit cards, promoting excessive consumption.

Avoiding the Debt Trap

Credit cards come with an obvious danger: debt accumulation. According to the Reserve Bank of Australia, the average credit card holder in Australia carries over $2,900 in debt. Even small balances, if unpaid, can accrue high-interest charges (often 15-25% annually), quickly snowballing into burdensome debt.

Over long period, this can translate into thousands—if not tens of thousands—of dollars paid in interest alone. In contrast, debit card users spend only what they already have. This simple rule can be one of the most effective ways to live within your means and avoid the mental, emotional, and financial stress of long-term debt.

Clarity and Simplicity in Budgeting

When managing daily expenses, simplicity is an asset. Debit cards give a clear picture of spending since transactions are instantly reflected in your bank balance. This transparency makes budgeting and financial planning easier. There are no statements with minimum payments, no interest calculations, and no worries about missing payment deadlines.

Over time, this clarity allows for better tracking of expenses and helps cultivate responsible money habits. You start to understand your true cost of living, which empowers you to make informed decisions about savings, investments, or reducing unnecessary expenses.

The Long-Term Benefits of debit cards

Using debit cards exclusively for two decades can yield substantial financial and personal benefits. Let us explore these with some projections and examples.

- Avoiding Interest Payments - Suppose an average credit card user pays $500 annually in interest (a conservative figure). Over 20 years, that is $10,000 saved, not counting fees or penalties. If that amount was invested with a modest 5% annual return, it could grow to over $17,000.
- Reduced Fees and Penalties - Late payment fees, annual fees, and over-limit charges can add up. By using a debit card, you bypass these hidden costs. Many debit cards have no annual fees and offer transaction fee-free usage if within the same bank network.
- Better Credit Alternatives - While credit cards can help build a credit score, so can on-time payment of other loans like student loans, mortgages, or even secured personal loans. You do not need to rely on a credit

card to establish a healthy credit profile, especially if you are not planning to borrow frequently.

- Emotional Peace - Living debt-free or with minimal debt leads to lower stress levels. The anxiety tied to monthly bills, rising interest, or potential default does not plague debit card users. Peace of mind is a priceless long-term benefit.
- Spending Awareness & Smart Consumption - Over time, debit card users tend to become more mindful of consumption patterns. Because every dollar spent is felt in real-time, the tendency to question purchases becomes second nature. This mindfulness can compound into substantial savings.

Addressing the Credit Card Reward Argument

Many argue that credit card rewards—such as cashback, points, or airline miles—make them worthwhile. While these perks are real, they often incentivize more spending. A 1-2% cashback is meaningless if it leads to 10-20% overspending.

Also, many debit cards now come with basic rewards or cashback options, and BNPL (Buy Now Pay Later) and fintech tools are also helping users earn perks without the risk of revolving debt.

Overall, choosing to use debit cards over credit cards for daily expenses is not merely about avoiding debt—it is a lifestyle choice that encourages discipline, transparency, and financial independence. Over a long period, the cumulative benefits—monetary and psychological—are enormous.

While credit cards have their place when used with exceptional discipline, most people struggle with delayed payment psychology and the temptation of high credit limits. By using a debit card, you are aligning your spending habits with your actual financial capacity, a choice that promotes sustainable, healthy financial habits.

The debit cards have worked extremely well for us, and this decision reflects our mindset: one that values living within our means, avoiding debt traps, and building wealth steadily and confidently.

Paying upfront where possible

Over the years, we have made a conscious effort to buy things with upfront payment whenever possible. Whether it was paying school fees, buying a car, or even making smaller purchases like electronics or furniture, we have usually preferred to pay the full amount rather than go down the path of instalments, loans, or credit cards. Some might say that it ties up cash or limits flexibility, but in our experience, the long-term benefits have far outweighed any short-term inconveniences.

One of the biggest and most obvious benefits of paying upfront is avoiding interest charges. As simple as it sounds, this alone can save you hundreds or even thousands of dollars over time. When you buy something on credit or through a loan, you are not just paying for the item—you are also paying extra for the “privilege” of spreading out the payments. That extra bit is interest, and it adds up quickly. It is easy to ignore when the monthly payments seem small, but when you look at the total cost over the years, it becomes clear how much more you're actually paying. By paying upfront, we have cut out that extra cost entirely. What we pay is exactly what it costs—nothing more, nothing less.

Another great advantage of upfront payment is the ability to negotiate a better deal. This is something people do not often realise. When you are ready to pay the full amount on the spot, it gives you power as a buyer. Sellers are often more willing to drop the price, offer a discount, or add a few bonuses just to seal the deal quickly. We found that when we bought our cars, as we were paying full amounts, we were able to save A$2000-4,000 on each traction. It is a win-win—you are helping them with quick cash flow, and in return, you save money. We have experienced this many times, whether it was buying a used car from a private seller or negotiating with a tradesperson for home repairs. A firm offer with cash, or upfront payment can often speak louder than a higher offer tied to future payments or financing.

There is also a mental and emotional relief that comes with paying upfront. When something is fully paid for, it is yours—free and clear. You do not have to think about monthly payments, upcoming deductions from your account, or due dates. There is no fear of missing a payment or incurring penalties. That mental space adds up to a less stressful financial life. It may not seem like a big deal when you only have one or two monthly commitments, but once you start stacking loans, credit cards, subscriptions, and instalment plans, your finances start to feel like a juggling act. Paying upfront simplifies all that. You know exactly where you stand, and it helps you stay in control.

Upfront payments also encourage better financial discipline. If you know you need to pay the full amount right away, you are more likely to think carefully about the purchase. It forces you to evaluate your priorities: Do I really need this? Can I afford it right now? Is there a better option? This kind of thinking helps avoid impulse buys and unnecessary spending. On the other hand, buying things on credit often removes that sense of caution—it is easy to think, "I will deal with it later," and by the time you realise how much you have spent, it is too late.

We also found that paying upfront helped us manage our household budget more effectively. For instance, when our boys were in private secondary schools, we always made sure to pay the annual fees in full at the beginning of the year. Not only did we save about 5% in early payment discounts, but we also

did not have to worry about term-by-term payments, which can be easy to forget and stressful to manage. That small discount—about $1,000 a year for both boys—was not massive, but it was still a worthwhile saving. More importantly, it allowed us to plan our year's cash flow more confidently. With school fees already taken care of, we could focus on other financial goals like investing, saving, or even taking a holiday without the constant worry of upcoming bills.

There is also something to be said about the sense of ownership that comes with paying upfront. Whether it is a car, a laptop, or a household appliance, it just feels better to know that it is fully yours from day one. There is a different mindset that comes with owning something outright versus knowing you are still paying it off. That mindset often brings a sense of pride and responsibility—you tend to take better care of things and make more thoughtful choices.

Another advantage is the psychological boost of outright ownership. When you pay for something in full, you own it free and clear—no bank, credit card company, or lender has a claim on it. This sense of ownership can be incredibly satisfying, whether it is a new phone, a piece of furniture, or even a home. There is no nagging worry about repossession or defaulting on payments. For example, buying a car outright means you do not have to stress about the bank repossessing it if you hit a rough patch financially. This peace of mind can make the purchase feel more rewarding and allows you to fully enjoy the item without the shadow of debt looming over you.

Paying upfront can also protect you from the risks associated with financing agreements. Many financing plans come with fine print that can trap unwary consumers—think balloon payments, adjustable interest rates, or clauses that penalize you for paying off the loan early. By paying upfront, you avoid these potential pitfalls entirely. You are not locked into a long-term commitment, and you do not have to worry about the terms of a contract changing or unexpected fees cropping up. This is particularly important in today's economy, where interest rates can fluctuate, and economic uncertainty can make long-term financial commitments feel risky.

Additionally, upfront payments can be a strategic move for building financial discipline. Saving up to pay for something in full requires planning, patience, and prioritization—skills that translate to other areas of personal finance. Instead of impulsively buying something on credit, you are forced to set a goal, budget for it, and wait until you have the funds. This process can help you develop better money management habits and reduce reliance on credit, which is a major step toward long-term financial stability. Over time, this discipline can lead to greater savings, fewer financial emergencies, and a stronger sense of control over your economic future.

Of course, we understand that not everyone has the flexibility to pay upfront for everything, especially with larger purchases like homes. But even in those cases, making a larger deposit or extra repayments early on can have similar benefits—lower interest over time, reduced loan duration, and improved financial peace of mind.

In the end, paying upfront has been a part of our broader financial philosophy: live within your means, spend slowly, and make thoughtful decisions. It is a simple principle, but over time, it has helped us stay debt-free, reduce financial stress, and build a solid foundation for our future. It may not always be the flashiest or most convenient option, but it is one that has worked well for us.

Beating Our Own Budget – A Simple Path to Savings and Growth

This has been one of the strategies that we have used early part of our financial journey – we would have approximate budget for shopping but always made sure we spent less than what we budgeted. Although thoughtful spending has become our second nature, we do not need this strategy anymore as we feel considerable financial security now.

In the early stages of a financial journey, establishing a budget is a foundational step toward achieving stability and long-term wealth. A budget provides a roadmap for managing income, expenses, and savings, ensuring that essential needs are met while setting aside resources for future goals. However, one of the most empowering and practical approaches to budgeting is not just sticking to it but *beating* it—spending less than planned by finding bargains and making savvy financial choices. This concept of "beating the budget" can significantly accelerate savings, fuel investments, and foster financial growth. Below, we explore how this strategy works, why it is effective, and how it can transform one's financial trajectory over time.

Budgeting is often viewed as a restrictive process, a set of rules to limit spending and curb impulses. However, a shift in perspective can make budgeting an exciting challenge, particularly when the goal is to spend less than allocated for essential items. Essential expenses typically include housing, utilities, groceries, transportation, and healthcare—categories that form the backbone of daily life. By setting realistic yet flexible budgets for these necessities, individuals create a framework where they can exercise creativity and resourcefulness to come in under budget.

Beating the budget does not mean compromising on quality or living a spartan lifestyle. Instead, it involves strategic decision-making, such as seeking out discounts, comparing prices, or adopting cost-effective habits. For example, buying in bulk, choosing generic brands, or negotiating service contracts can reduce costs without sacrificing needs. The savings generated from these efforts can then be redirected toward investments, emergency funds, or other financial goals, creating a positive feedback loop of financial discipline and growth.

One of the most effective ways to beat the budget is by becoming an adept bargain hunter. Bargains are opportunities to acquire goods or services at a lower cost than anticipated, whether through sales, coupons, second-hand purchases, or loyalty programs. For instance, grocery shopping can be optimized by planning meals around seasonal produce, using apps to find digital coupons, or shopping at discount stores. Similarly, utilities and subscriptions can often be negotiated or switched to more affordable providers, reducing monthly bills.

The psychological reward of finding a bargain is significant. It transforms budgeting from a chore into a game, where each dollar saved feels like a small victory. Over time, these small wins accumulate, leading to substantial savings. The true power of beating the budget lies in what happens to the savings. Rather than letting the extra money sit idly in a checking account or be absorbed into discretionary spending, intentional redirection of these funds can amplify financial growth. Moreover, beating the budget creates a buffer for unexpected expenses, reducing reliance on credit cards or loans during emergencies. This financial cushion enhances security and prevents debt accumulation, which can derail long-term goals.

Consistently beating the budget has fostered financial discipline in us. Although we do not strictly follow budgets anymore, it has helped us in our long-term success.

Over time, the habit of beating the budget compounds its benefits. The savings accrued can be invested to generate passive income, reduce financial stress, and provide the freedom to pursue opportunities like career changes or early retirement. For example, redirecting $100 a month into an investment account with an average annual return of 7% could grow to over $15,000 in 10 years, demonstrating the power of consistent, small savings.

Moreover, this approach instils a mindset of resourcefulness and resilience. Economic challenges, such as inflation or job loss, become less daunting when one has a track record of finding creative ways to save. It also aligns with the broader principle of living below one's means, a cornerstone of financial independence.

Looking back now, this simple habit – something as basic as spending less than we intended to – was foundational to our financial success. It did not require a degree in finance or access to complicated investment tools. It just required discipline, awareness, and a willingness to question every expense.

Cheap phone and Internet plans and not subscribing pay TV

Cheap cell phone plans

In today's digital world, mobile phones and internet access are necessities. But necessity does not mean we have to go overboard with spending. From the very beginning, we have believed in making practical, informed financial decisions, and our choice of mobile phone and internet plans reflects this mindset. Throughout our working life, we have avoided expensive contracts and high-end telecom providers, opting instead for low-cost, prepaid mobile services. This decision, though simple, has saved us thousands over the years and kept our financial life free of unnecessary burdens.

When we first arrived in Australia, we noticed how many people were locked into expensive mobile phone contracts. Major telecom companies would often offer the latest smartphone bundled into a 24-month plan, which appeared attractive at first. However, a closer look revealed that these plans came with significant hidden costs, interest-like pricing structures, and limited flexibility.

Instead of signing up for these plans, we took a different path. We chose prepaid mobile plans—starting with Aldi Mobile, which offered a $12/month option that included more than enough data, calls, and texts for our everyday needs. Over the years, our average cost has been just $18 per person per month. For two people, that is $36 per month or $432 per year.

Another critical financial habit that helped us avoid unnecessary expenses was our decision to always buy our own mobile phones outright, rather than getting them as part of a mobile plan. Telecom providers are well known for marketing their plans with “free” or “discounted” handsets. But let us be honest—nothing is ever truly free. When you sign a contract that includes a handset, you’re essentially committing to paying off that device in instalments over 24 or 36 months, often with hidden fees or inflated plan prices. The handset might come with a locked-in price tag that is significantly higher than if you had purchased the phone directly from a retailer or a certified second-hand dealer. Furthermore, these plans often tempt people into buying higher-end models they do not really need, which leads to overspending. To some extent we were lucky as our phones were provided by our employer while we bought cheap phones for our children.

Our modest spending on phones and mobile data also meant that more of our income could be directed toward meaningful long-term goals: paying down the mortgage faster, saving for our children's education, investing in property, and building an emergency fund. These small monthly savings became part of a larger discipline that supported financial independence and peace of mind. We believe that over 25 years, by spending an average of $432 annually instead of $1,272, we saved a total of $21,000. That is just from mobile plans alone—without factoring in the additional savings from buying handsets outright.

The Power of Skipping Pay TV: A 25-Year Slow Spending Strategy

For over 25 years, we made a conscious decision never to subscribe to pay TV services such as Foxtel in Australia (in 2026, we do have several subscriptions which we only acquired about 5 years ago). At first glance, this might seem like a small, even insignificant choice. After all, what is $25 a month for a bit of entertainment? But when viewed through the lens of long-term financial discipline, this simple decision became a quiet but powerful pillar in our slow spending journey—and it paid off more than most people realise.

Let us do the math: $25 per month saved over 25 years equals $300 per year. Multiply that by 25 years and you have got $7,500. Now, factor in what could have happened if we invested that money instead—say in a modest-performing investment or even just a savings account with compound interest—and the final number could easily exceed $15,000. All from simply not subscribing to pay TV.

But the benefits go far beyond the dollars saved. By opting out of pay TV, we found ourselves with more time for meaningful activities—reading, learning new skills, exercising, spending quality time with family, or even starting side hustles. Instead of passively consuming whatever was on screen, we chose to live more intentionally.

This choice also helped us avoid the temptation of lifestyle inflation. Pay TV often comes bundled with additional costs—sports packages, streaming upgrades, box rentals, or even needing a bigger internet plan to support higher usage. It is a slippery slope, and we intentionally stayed off it. In hindsight, it was about more than money—it was about protecting our mindset from consumer culture and from believing that entertainment equals happiness.

We also discovered plenty of free or low-cost entertainment alternatives. Australia has excellent public broadcasting (like ABC and SBS), as well as libraries, YouTube, podcasts, and other digital resources that provide informative and engaging content at zero cost. Over time, we found that we did not miss pay TV at all. In fact, we valued our time more because it was not scheduled around television programs.

This one choice—no pay TV—also reinforced our financial discipline. It taught us to question recurring costs and to think long-term. When we applied the same principle to other areas—like limiting takeaway food, buying used cars, or avoiding unnecessary gadgets—the savings compounded further. These sacrifices were not about deprivation; they were about priorities. Each dollar saved on something unnecessary was a dollar we could invest in our future.

Ultimately, the decision to skip pay TV was not about television. It was about building a habit of delayed gratification, conscious spending, and valuing freedom over fleeting comfort. And today, as we enjoy financial freedom and a sense of control over our lives, we know it was sacrifices like this—small, consistent, and intentional—that helped us get here.

So next time someone says, "It is just $25 a month," remember: small leaks can sink big ships. And small savings, over time, can build a fortune.

Self-booking plane tickets and booking early

Living in Australia with family in Ireland and India means we're no strangers to long-haul flights and frequent travel. Over the years, we have racked up countless trips to visit loved ones, attend family reunions, and soak up some much-needed holiday time. But let us be real, travel is not cheap, especially when you are crossing continents regularly. Early on, we decided to take control of our travel planning by self-booking plane tickets instead of relying on travel agents. This choice, paired with our "**Slow Spending**" philosophy, has saved us a small fortune—probably over $10,000 in the past 25 years.

In our earlier time in New Zealand (early 1990s), we did us a travel agent to book our flights as that was the only way to book travel and our travel agent in Palmerston North was extremely friendly. The Internet was not permeated significantly in our lives and were unaware of anyone booking their flights independent of travel agents. When we first moved to Australia, we considered using travel agents to handle our bookings. It seemed convenient but we quickly realized that convenience comes at a cost, both in fees and in missing out on the best deals. Travel agents often charge service fees, and their recommendations might not always prioritize the cheapest or most flexible options. There is also a service fee if you want to make any changes if the flight is already booked. By self-booking, we cut out the middleman and gained the flexibility to hunt for the best prices and make changes to our plans without extra hassle or costs. Plus, there is something satisfying about knowing you have snagged a great deal on your own.

The cornerstone of our travel savings strategy has been booking early—sometimes *really* early, like six months or more in advance. This approach has been a gamechanger, especially for frequent domestic flights. Take Mary's weekly work trips from Melbourne to Sydney, for example. For six years, she had been flying this route about sixty times a year (return trips) for her job. By booking the budget airline, Jetstar flights well in advance, we managed to keep the cost per round trip on average around $100. If we waited until closer to the flight date, that same ticket could easily cost $220 each way—more than double! That is a savings of about $120 per trip. Multiply that by sixty trips a year (thirty return flights), and we are talking $7,200 saved annually. Over six years, that adds up to a whopping $43,200 just on domestic flights. Those saving were realised using a budget airline like Jetstar, imagine how much those will be if we had booked with the major airlines such as Qantas and Virgin – one could easily double that number.

The same logic applies to our international flights, including trips to India and Ireland. Booking flights to these destinations early has consistently saved us hundreds, if not thousands, per trip. Over 25 years, we estimate we have saved **over $20,000** on international travel alone by planning ahead and booking ourselves. Airlines like Qantas, Air India, Singapore Airlines, and Emirates often release their cheapest fares months in advance, so being able to book early has helped us. Once the flight booking is made, it gives us peace of mind and helps in planning trips efficiently.

Over time, we have realised that flight aggregator websites like Skyscanner, Kayak, and Google Flights can help find the best deals. These platforms are like treasure maps for budget travellers, pulling together prices from dozens of airlines and letting you compare options in seconds. We will usually start with Skyscanner to get a sense of the cheapest airlines and dates, then head straight to the airline's own website to book. Why? Because booking directly with the airline often means lower fees if you need to change or cancel your ticket later. For example, when planning a trip to India, we might use Skyscanner to spot a great fare on Singapore Airlines, then go to their website to finalize the booking. Same goes for trips to Ireland—aggregators help us narrow down options, but we always double-check the airline's site for any hidden discounts or better terms. This combo approach has helped us snag deals that travel agents might overlook.

One of the biggest perks of self-booking is the control it gives you. Most airlines have user-friendly online portals where you can tweak your itinerary, upgrade seats, or even cancel for a refund (if the fare allows). This flexibility has saved us not just money but also the headache of dealing with a third party.

No matter how carefully we plan, travel comes with risks—lost luggage, flight cancellations, medical emergencies, you name it. That is why we *always* **get travel insurance** for every trip. For a small premium—usually a fraction of the ticket cost—it is like a safety net that lets us travel with confidence. Whether it is a missed connection in Singapore or a sudden illness in Dublin, insurance has saved us from unexpected expenses more than once. It is a non-negotiable part of our travel strategy, and we would recommend it to anyone, especially for long-haul international trips.

Our travel habits are a big part of what we call "**Slow Spending**"—a mindset where we prioritize thoughtful, deliberate choices to stretch our dollars further and build wealth over time. By booking early, using aggregator sites, and managing our own bookings, we have turned travel from a budget-buster into an opportunity to save.

Staying in cheaper accommodation while travelling

Over the years, our family have had the opportunity to explore the world together, from the bustling cities of the US and the historic streets of Spain to the breathtaking landscapes of New Zealand, the unique culture of Japan, and the tropical paradise of Fiji. When we travel overseas, one of the biggest expenses after flights is accommodation. And like many others, we quickly learned that where you sleep at night does not have to be luxurious to be comfortable. Over the years, we have stayed in a range of places, but the ones that really stood out were not five-star hotels with champagne breakfasts—they were the humble, well-equipped, and homely Airbnbs or similar types of accommodations.

Whether we were in the U.S., Spain, New Zealand, Japan or Fiji, our choice to stay in modest, budget-friendly places helped us not only save money but also experience travel in a far more personal and memorable way.

The most obvious benefit of staying in a moderate Airbnb-style accommodation is the cost saving. Hotels, especially in major cities or tourist hotspots, can be extremely expensive. And even if they offer some luxuries like daily room service, plush robes, or fancy breakfast buffets, these perks do not always justify the high price tag—especially when you're out exploring most of the day.

With Airbnb, we have consistently paid less compared with nearby hotels, especially when booking early. That is a massive difference when you consider the total cost for a family over two or three weeks of travel. But what makes it better is that we do not have to compromise on the essentials: we always choose clean, well-located homes or apartments with good reviews and basic facilities like a kitchen, laundry, and Wi-Fi.

One of the features we look for in any place we book is a functional kitchen. Having a kitchen while travelling is an absolute gamechanger for us. Not only does it cut down drastically on food expenses, but it also makes travelling more relaxed and enjoyable, especially as a family.

Staying in a house or apartment rather than a hotel room gives you a more homely feel. After a long day exploring new cities, national parks, or historical sites, there is something comforting about returning "home" to a place that feels like more than just a room with a bed.

There is also the family dynamic to consider. In a hotel, everyone might be cramped into one or two beds, and there's little room for movement. But in an Airbnb, you can find places with separate bedrooms, living areas, and even outdoor space. Kids can have their own room, and we can have a proper meal together at a dining table rather than perching on a hotel bed with takeaway containers.

One of the hidden gems of staying in these types of accommodations is the opportunity to live like a local. Hotels are usually located in busy tourist areas, but Airbnbs are often nestled in real neighbourhoods. This gives you a chance to see a different side of the country—the morning walks of locals, the nearby bakeries, the tiny parks where children play, and the corner stores that do not appear on travel guides.

Another benefit is the flexibility. With most Airbnb-type stays, there is no rigid schedule for meals, no waiting for housekeeping, and no need to tip every time you need something. You are free to wake up late, eat breakfast in your pyjamas, or do laundry whenever you like. This especially helps when dealing with jet lag or adjusting to a new time zone.

We also enjoy the sense of independence and self-reliance that comes from managing our own space while travelling. It is a small thing, but being able to wash your own clothes during long trips is not just convenient—it also means you can pack lighter and save on checked baggage fees.

Savings on cars

Buying demo cars

A demo car (short for "demonstration") is a vehicle that has been used by the dealership for display or test-drive purposes. These cars are typically in excellent condition, with low kilometres on the odometer, and still fall under the manufacturer's warranty. In most cases, they have never been registered to a private owner, meaning you're still technically the first owner. They may have a few hundred to a few thousand kilometres on them, but they are far from being used or old. In many cases, they have just been sitting in the showroom or used occasionally for short test drives. But what makes them attractive is the price.

Here are the main reasons we think buying a demo car is a smart move:

- There is significant cost advantage in buying a demo car. Demo models can be discounted by thousands of dollars. The car is technically new—has not had a previous owner—but because it has already been driven a little and cannot be sold as "new-new," the dealership must lower the price. You are getting nearly all the perks of a new car but at a used car price.
- Most demo vehicles are still covered by the full manufacturer's warranty, starting from the date of your purchase. You do not lose the protection or benefits that come with a new car, even though someone else may have driven it for 500 or 2000 kilometres.
- Demo models often come loaded with extras—think upgraded trim, leather seats, or advanced safety features—because dealerships want to showcase the best versions of their cars for test drives. So sometimes, you end up with a higher-spec car than what you were originally looking for, for the same or even lower price.
- If you are ordering a new car, especially in recent years with global supply chain issues, you might have to wait weeks or even months for delivery. With demo cars, they are already at the dealership and ready to go. You

can drive them off the lot often the same week you buy them.

- Because demo cars have been used (even lightly), dealerships are usually more open to negotiating on price. They want to move these cars quickly to make space for newer stock. You can sometimes score additional accessories or better financing options as part of the deal.

Apart from buying second-hand cars in earlier part of our career, we've bought three new demo cars, each time saving thousands of dollars compared to a new model straight off the production line:

1. **Hyundai 3-door Hatchback** We decided to buy a small hatchback for city driving. Instead of going for the typical 5-door model, we chose a 3-door version. That decision alone saved us about **$5000**. We did not mind having two fewer doors since it was our secondary car. The car was new, clean, and came with all the modern features we needed—without the extra cost.

2. **Mercedes-Benz Demo Model** When we were ready to buy a more premium car, we investigated Mercedes-Benz options. Instead of choosing a factory-order vehicle, we picked a demo model that had just a few thousand kilometres on it. The dealer had used it for customer test drives, and it was in pristine condition. Because it was technically "used" by the dealership, we saved a whopping

$8000. All the features, full warranty, and new car feel—just without the hefty price tag.

3. **Renault Koleos Demo SUV**
   For our family trips and longer drives, we wanted a solid SUV. Again, we went with a demo version of the Renault Koleos. It had already done a couple of thousand kilometres but was still in fantastic condition. By avoiding a brand-new version of the same car, we managed to save another **$8000**. That saving alone covered several months of fuel, insurance, and registration costs. Moreover, the car came with preinstalled tow bar and a roof rack which could have cost another $4000.

Buying demo cars has helped us strike a perfect balance between getting the benefits of a new vehicle—reliability, safety, technology, and warranty—while still staying within a sensible budget. In our case, just with three cars, we estimate total savings of **over $21,000**. That is money we were able to put into other financial goals—investments, travel, or even paying down the mortgage faster. It is not always about getting the cheapest car—it's about getting the smartest deal. Demo cars gave us that little sweet spot between quality and affordability, and we are better off for it. Whether you are buying your first vehicle or upgrading your family car, take a serious look at demo models. You might just drive away with a great deal and a big smile.

Buying fuel at the lower price end of the cycle

In Australia, there are weekly/fortnightly/monthly variations in the petrol price, and we have mostly bought at lower end of the price cycle. Whenever, we have been caught at the higher end of price cycle, we fill the tank just enough to last until the next lower end of the price cycle. The savings vary from city to city but in Melbourne come around $333 per year. Over, 20 years this saving can amount to $6660.

Servicing car at an alternative garage

When it comes to maintaining our cars, we have always believed in keeping things practical and smart. Over the years, we have owned several vehicles – from a Daewoo Nubira in our early days in Australia to newer models like a Mercedes and a Renault Koleos. But one thing has remained consistent: we have never been in a hurry to get our cars serviced at the big-name manufacturer dealerships.

We have always found that those dealership garages, while very polished and professional-looking, charge a hefty premium – sometimes unnecessarily. Of course, they claim it is for genuine parts, trained staff, and brand standards. But we quickly realised that we could get equally reliable servicing done elsewhere, for much less.

Instead of handing our cars over to dealership service centres, we found a reliable local garage that understood cars just as well – sometimes even better. Over time, they became our go-to for all things related to car maintenance. Whether it was regular servicing, logbook stamps, oil changes, brake pads, or just general check-ups, they took care of it all.

On average, servicing a car at a manufacturer dealership can be quite expensive – especially if it is a European make like Mercedes. We have seen quotes as high as $900 to $1,200 for a single standard service. In contrast, our independent mechanic does a thorough logbook service for around $300 to $400. Multiply that by two cars, and you are looking at savings of roughly $1,000 to $2,000 a year – just on routine maintenance.

Let us say we have saved about $2,000 per year by avoiding dealership servicing for both cars. Over the past 20 years, that adds up to a massive $40,000. It is quite amazing when you think about it – $40,000 is the price of a brand-new car! Or it could be a deposit on an investment property. It could be a major family holiday or even a decent chunk toward retirement savings. And all that from just being sensible about car servicing. Once you develop the habits of slow spending these tricks come naturally to you.

Another benefit of sticking with a smaller garage is the personal touch. Over time, our mechanic got to know us and our cars. They would often point out things we could keep an eye on before they became a problem. Unlike some dealerships that are notorious for upselling unnecessary work, our mechanic was upfront. If something did not need to be fixed immediately, they would tell us. That kind of honesty is priceless.

We have also found that turnaround times are often better with independent garages. Dealerships usually have a long queue, and you might need to wait days just to get a booking.

With our mechanic, we could often call in the morning and get the car looked at the same or next day.

Then there is the convenience and location factor. Dealerships are often located in industrial areas or further out of town. Getting there, arranging a lift back, and waiting for your car to be ready can be a hassle. Our local garage is just a short drive away, and they even offer a courtesy car if needed.

One of the concerns people often raise is about warranty – especially when the car is new. But here is the thing: as long as the servicing is done by a qualified mechanic and follows the manufacturer's logbook guidelines, your warranty remains valid. This is something many people do not know. The Australian Competition and Consumer Commission (ACCC) has clear guidelines on this. So even during the warranty period of our newer cars, we stuck to our independent mechanic – and never had a problem.

As a part of **slow spending**, saving $40,000 over 20 years has been huge for us. Our cars are still running great, and we have extra cash for whatever life throws our way. It just shows you do not need to spend big to take care of your cars. If you are sick of those dealership bills, give a local garage a shot—you might end up with better service and a way happier bank account.

Cooking at home and eating less out

Over the years, we have noticed something about ourselves—something quite simple but surprisingly powerful. We genuinely prefer home-cooked meals to eating out. It is not that we never dine out or do not enjoy a nice restaurant experience occasionally, but day-to-day, we get much more satisfaction from preparing and eating our meals at home. This habit, though rooted in personal preference, has turned out to be one of the smartest choices we have made for our finances, health, and family life.

Let us start with the most obvious benefit—financial savings. Eating out, whether it is at a fancy restaurant or a casual café, adds up quickly. A typical restaurant meal for two people can easily cost $50 or more, even without drinks or dessert. Compare that to a home-cooked meal where you can prepare something hearty and delicious for under $15 for the whole family. Over a week, which is a savings of hundreds of dollars, and over a year, we are talking thousands.

Australian households spend a sizeable portion of their food budget on dining out. According to industry research, household expenditure on eating out increased by over 20% between 2009 and 2019, with the average household now allocating more than one-third of its food budget to dining out. More recent data suggests that individuals spend an average of $52 per week on eating out, with younger generations being more likely to dine out compared to older Australians. Additionally, Australian households spend approximately $198 per week on hotels, cafes, and restaurants, making it one of the top expenses in household budgets. On average, for 25 years the cost of eating out comes to $257,400 ($198x52x13). As a family. we on average eat out 5 times year (birthdays and Mother's Day) spending about $400 each time making it $50,000 ($400x5x25). This means we are saving **$207,400 over 25 years**.

But it is not just about the money. Health is another major benefit. When we cook at home, we control what goes into our food. There are no hidden sugars or excess salt. Eating out often means consuming more calories, unhealthy fats, and oversized portions—things that can affect long-term health. With home cooking, we can balance our meals better, and over time, which reflects in our overall well-being.

Another benefit is the family connection. When we cook and eat at home, it becomes more than just a meal—its time spent together. Whether we are preparing food as a couple or as a whole family, it becomes a shared activity. Our kids have learned the basics of cooking just by watching and helping. They also appreciate food more because they see the effort that goes into preparing it. Sitting down together for a meal encourages conversation and bonding—something that is hard to come by when everyone is glued to their devices or rushing around during the week.

Home cooking also helps reduce waste and unnecessary consumption. When we cook at home, we tend to plan better. We use our leftovers, repurpose ingredients, and avoid over-ordering. At restaurants, it is easy to overestimate how hungry you are and end up leaving food behind—or forcing yourself to finish it, which is not ideal either. Cooking at home has taught us the value of food, and we are more conscious of how much we buy and use.

And let us not forget the emotional satisfaction that comes from cooking. There is something grounding about chopping vegetables, stirring a simmering sauce, or baking a fresh loaf of bread. It is therapeutic in a way. It gives us a sense of control and accomplishment, especially after a long workday. The smell of home-cooked food wafting through the house is comforting and welcoming. It makes a house feel like a home.

As the birthdays of our two boys fall within 3 weeks of each other, we have been able to celebrate with a combined birthday party for several years, thus making some small savings. When our boys were young, for most birthdays, Mary made the cake at home rather than buying from a cake shop.

Bringing lunch to work

One of the strategies (more as habits) for us have been bringing our own lunch from home to our work. Bringing your own lunch to work is a habit that might seem small at first, but over time—especially for a couple who have stuck with it for decades—it can lead to some pretty amazing results, both financially and personally.

This is one simple habit that quietly worked in our favour over the last 30 years. Nothing fancy—sometimes just a leftover curry, sometimes a humble sandwich and fruit—but we stuck to it. Day after day, year after year. While colleagues were lining up at food courts or ordering Uber Eats, we were sitting at our desks or in the staff room, happily eating from our lunchboxes. And let us tell you—it has paid off. Big time.

It might seem like a small thing, but over three decades, the financial and health benefits have really added up. And best of all, it did not feel like a sacrifice. In fact, it became a part of our lifestyle—normal, easy, and even enjoyable.

We did not start bringing lunch for some grand financial reason. It was only common sense. In the early days, when we were new to Australia and settling into jobs, every dollar counted. Eating out every day was not even on our radar—we simply did not have the money for that kind of luxury. So, we did what we always had done back home: made food at home, packed it up, and took it with us.

Soon, it became a habit. And the more we looked around, the more we noticed that people were spending quite a bit every day on takeaway lunches. At first, it was just surprising. But over time, we realised: this one small decision—just bringing lunch—was making a huge difference to our bottom line.

Suppose someone buys lunch at work—a sandwich, a drink, maybe a snack. Easily around $12 to $20, depending on what and where. Let us take a middle-ground figure: $15 per day. Assuming there are 240 working days, the cost will come to $3600 per year per person or $7200 for two people. This could add up to **$216,000** over 30 years of working life! That is the price of a whole house deposit in some places! And we are not even counting the interest or potential investment return if we had put that money into a savings account or shares. The financial numbers are impressive, but that is not the only benefit. Bringing your own lunch gives you full control over what you eat. No hidden sugars, excess fats, or overly salty food. You choose the ingredients, the portion sizes, and how much oil or butter goes in.

There is something comforting about knowing what is in your food. Packing lunch was not just about saving money—it turned into a rhythm in our lives. We cooked more at home in general, since we knew leftovers could be used the next day. This naturally reduced our reliance on takeaway dinners too, which is another bonus for the budget.

Bringing your own lunch is a perfect example of "**slow spending**"—a financial strategy that focuses on making small, sustainable changes to your daily habits to achieve big results over time. It is not about depriving yourself or living a life of austerity; it is about being mindful of where your money goes and finding ways to redirect it toward things that truly matter to you.

Dietary habits - Being vegetarian and non-drinkers helped us in slow spending

This is something that we did not expect to happen as we were both eating meat before meeting each other. Alcohol was never part of our lives. These habits inadvertently have helped our "Slow Spending" philosophy.

Being vegetarian

We have been vegetarians for over 30 years now—not because it was trendy or because we followed some celebrity's diet advice. It was just how it happened for us. Both Ranjan (non-beef) and Mary ate meat until just after our marriage in 1994. One day, suddenly Mary decided in later part of 1994 that we would stop eating meat, *i.e.* no beef, lamb, chicken or seafood, *i.e.* become vegetarians. For Ranjan, who grew up on predominantly vegetarian diet, it was not a problem at all. While growing up in India, he hardly had meat as it was considerably expensive than vegetables, beans and pulses. Meat was only offered in the family on special occasions, such as birthdays and weddings.

Over time, we found that this lifestyle not only kept us feeling healthy and light, but it also ended up saving us a good chunk of money. And when we look back, we realise how much it supported our "**Slow Spending**" strategy over the years. We were not always vegetarian, not until we got married in 1994. While growing up in Ireland, Mary had a typical western diet – meat and three veges. Ranjan's diet consisted of mainly vegetarian foods with occasional chicken through curries or fast-food restaurants.

The Cost of Vegetarian vs. Non-Vegetarian Meals: What the Data Says

First off, let us talk about the grocery bill. Meat is often the priciest item in the cart, so cutting it out naturally trims the total. A 2021 study from Oxford University found that in high-income countries like the US, vegan diets can slash food costs by up to one-third compared to meat-heavy diets. Vegetarian diets are a close second, saving nearly as much. If you are spending, say, $300 a month on groceries for a typical omnivore diet, going vegetarian could drop that to around $200–$225. That is $75–$100 saved monthly, or $900–$1,200 a year.

Another study, published in 2023 by the Physicians Committee for Responsible Medicine, showed that a low-fat vegan diet cuts food costs by 16%, or about $500 a year, compared to a diet with meat and dairy. Even accounting for slightly higher spending on veggies and legumes, the savings from ditching animal products are clear.

A 2025, a US report by CouponBirds broke it down further, looking at weekly grocery shops at stores like Walmart and Kroger. They found that a vegetarian diet saves an average of $32.59 per week—$130.36 a month—compared to an unrestricted diet. Swapping salmon for tofu, for example, saves $6.31 per meal.

Real-world folks back this up too. Toni Okamoto, who runs the blog *Plant-Based on a Budget*, says her clients spend $40–$50 a week per person on plant-based groceries, way less than the average meat-eater's bill. One person who switched to a plant-heavy diet saved $800 over five months.

As we reflect on our journey, being vegetarian has been more than just a dietary choice. It has been a quiet enabler of financial stability, health, and long-term wealth creation. It fit so seamlessly into our Slow Spending lifestyle that we hardly noticed it working in the background. But looking back over 30+ years, the impact is undeniable.

Being vegetarian may not be applicable to most of the people, but it inadvertently has worked out for us.

Not drinking alcohol

In addition to being vegetarians, we are also non-drinkers which has also helped our bottom-line too. In Australia, drinking alcohol is a common social habit, but it is also an expensive one. A single glass of wine in a restaurant can easily cost $10–$15. A bottle of decent wine from a store might be $20–$30. A pint of beer at a pub? Around $10. Whiskey and spirits are even more expensive, especially when consumed out.

Let us take a modest drinking example for an average couple: two bottles of wine per week (one each over dinner or shared across days) at $20 each = $40/week; two beers per person per week (one casual pub visit or with a meal) at $10 each = $40/week; occasional whiskey/spirits, let's say $10/week average over the year; that adds up to $90/week, which is $4,680/year. Over 30 years, this amounts to $4,680 x 30 = $140,400! And that is a conservative estimate. Many people spend far more, especially those who drink socially, go to pubs regularly, or enjoy cocktails, champagne, or premium alcohol.

This is not unique to Australia. In the US, average households spend about $500–$1,000 per year per adult on alcohol, depending on habits and lifestyle. In the UK and Ireland, it is common for a weekly pub night to cost $30–$50 or more for a couple. Over decades, that's tens of thousands of dollars or pounds that quietly trickle out of household budgets.

Shopping a cheaper supermarket

Wherever we lived, we have always tried to find a supermarket that is cheaper than main supermarkets. While living in New Zealand, we used to shop at a supermarket called Pak'n Save which was considerably cheaper than New World and Woolworths. In Denmark, our supermarkets of choice were Netto, Aldi and Lidl, but we occasionally shopped at premium supermarkets like Irma and Fotex.

That habit continued for us in Australia. Although we initially shopped at Woolworths with all the vegetables shopping carried out in bulk in a cheap shop run by a Lebanese family in Werribee. When the German cheap supermarket Aldi (a competitor to Lidl in Europe) was launched in our neighbourhood, we were quick to adopt shopping there. We immediately noticed weekly saving when we switched from Woolworths to Aldi. Keeping up our slow spending theme, we now mostly shop at Aldi with occasional visits to Woolworths and Coles supermarkets in our neighbourhood.

Here we have tried to estimate the savings that would have been made by shopping at Aldi. A consumer advocacy group, Choice Australia has compared the prices of the following fourteen essential items major supermarkets in Australia: milk, butter, bread, apples, carrots, frozen peas, Weetbix, mincemeat, penne pasta, diced tomatoes canned, block of cheese, flour, tea bags and sugar.

The price comparison from three major supermarkets in December 2024, in Australia is show here.

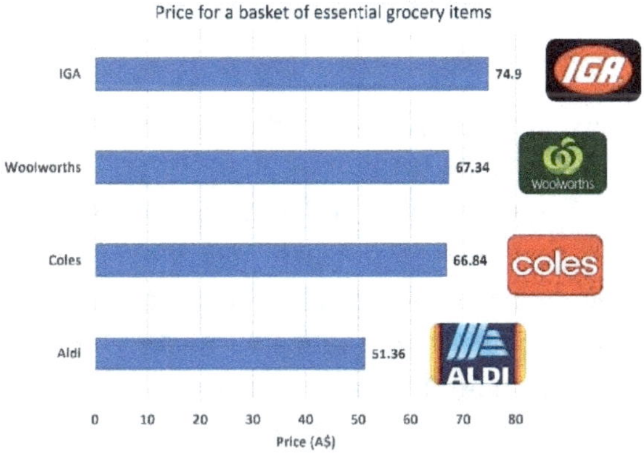

Figure 7: Price comparison of a basket of fourteen essential food items among three major supermarkets in Australia (data from the supermarket survey in December 2024 by Choice magazine Australia)

The results from the survey comparing fourteen essential grocery items in Aldi, Coles, Woolworths and IGA suggests that ALDI is 30% cheaper that the two major supermarkets (Coles and Woolworths) and 45% cheaper than the independent supermarket (IGA) when essential food items are compared.

According to Finder.com.au, the average Australian household spends around $204 per week on groceries. This amount can vary depending on household size, location, and spending habits. For example, families with two adults and two children typically spend between $280 and $400 per week on groceries. If we assume on average, Australian family spends

$300 per week on grocery ($15,600 per year), the total spend over 25 years comes to $390,000. As we mostly shop at Aldi for groceries, simple calculations on **our savings in grocery bill over 25 years comes to $117,000** (30% cheaper at Aldi supermarket).

When buying grocery items, we always look for unit price rather than just the price of an item. For examples, if fresh tomatoes come two different forms, a prepacked and a loose form. On surface, the prepack may look convenient and appealing, however, we convert the price of each to a unit price such as per Kg, the prepack usually comes out more expensive to buy. This also applies to single pack and multipacks offered for various products, multipack often turns out to be cheaper on per unit basis. We have often bought some grocery items in bulk, especially those, shelf-stable, long-life products such as canned food, pulses, oils *etc*.

Multiple sources of income

For over 15 years, while being employed fulltime, Ranjan been publishing a market intelligence Newsletter "Functional Foods Weekly" as a side hustle, generating $30,000-$40,000 per year. This involved spending time after work, and weekends, going through various online resources, and compiling into a comprehensive weekly digest. The Digest was popular among major food companies around the world. Although we paid higher taxes with extra income, it was still financially worthwhile. A simple calculation can show that this generated extra $450,000-$600,000 (before tax) over 15 years.

Superannuation through self-managed superfund

Compulsory superannuation in Australia, known as the Superannuation Guarantee (SG), was introduced in 1992. This legislation mandated employers to make contributions to their employees' superannuation funds, significantly expanding retirement savings for Australian workers. Prior to 1992, while superannuation existed, it was not compulsory for all employees. The SG aimed to address the challenge of retirement income by ensuring almost all workers had some form of savings for their post-work life. The initial contribution rate was 3% (or 4% for larger employers), and this has gradually increased over time, currently standing at 12% in 2025.

Superannuation in Australia is an effective way to save for retirement, with tax benefits designed to encourage long-term savings. Your super contributions are generally taxed at a concessional rate of 15%, which is often lower than your regular income tax rate. If you are 60 or older, withdrawals from your super are typically tax-free. Additionally, investment earnings within your super fund are taxed at a maximum of 15%, making it a tax-efficient way to grow your retirement savings. We caught up on nitty gritty of this very quickly after arriving in Australia

When we arrived in Australia in February 2001 (Age 38 and 35), we started with $0 in the superannuation account. At the time, employers contributed 9% of the salary into our superannuation accounts. This is called the concessional contribution and taxed at concessional rate of 15% which was significantly lower than approximately 36% on our salary.

However, to encourage savings there is a provision in Australia to top up your superannuation by pre-tax, voluntary contribution which is also taxed at the concessional rate of 15%. The total amount (employer and voluntary) should not exceed a predetermined amount. If it exceeded the maximum amount, there are large tax penalties.

Voluntary contribution to the superannuation to the superannuation not only boosted our superannuation balances, but it also reduced the amount of tax payable each month. The concessional superannuation cap in 2001 to 2011, was A$25,000 per person. This included employer contribution (9 to 9.5%) plus our voluntary pre-tax contributions.

Each year we voluntarily contributed as much as we could to the allowed maximum of $25,000 each. At the time we had two small children needed childcare at approximately A10,000 each per year.

Our superannuation funds were held and managed separately and managed by different funds. Ranjan's superannuation was managed by AMP Super and Mary's by Plum Super.

In 2011, when we set up self-managed superannuation fund (SMSF), we had pooled money of A$328,00. Which means over the 20 year, if our employers contributed A$360,000 (A$9,000 each per year), we were able to voluntarily contribute A$296,000, **saving us A$62,160 in tax**. Although, this is a simplified calculation, it nevertheless, highlights the importance of sacrifices and disciplined spendings on our part.

A self-managed super fund (SMSF) is exactly what it sounds like—a super fund that you manage yourself, rather than letting a big company like AMP or Plum manage it for you. Running an SMSF is not for everyone. But for us, it made a lot of sense as we set up with Esuperfund which had low annual fee of $699 when we joined in 2011. The advantages of having a SMSF is that you control how the funds are invested. Most of our SMSF was used to buy 2 properties while small amounts were used for term deposits and shares on Australian Stock Exchange.

To demonstrate the growth of our self-managed superfund (SMSF), we created a simple bar graph showing the yearly value of our SMSF from 2011 to 2024. It is not flashy, but it is real. Each year, the balance in our fund grew—not always dramatically, but consistently. There were some standout years, especially after 2017, when the growth picked up pace. Part of this was due to stronger investment returns and partly because we were regularly making extra contributions, over and above the compulsory employer payments.

What you see in the graph is the power of compounding combined with **slow spending and smart saving**. While others may have been upgrading cars or chasing risky investments, we were topping up our superannuation bit by bit.

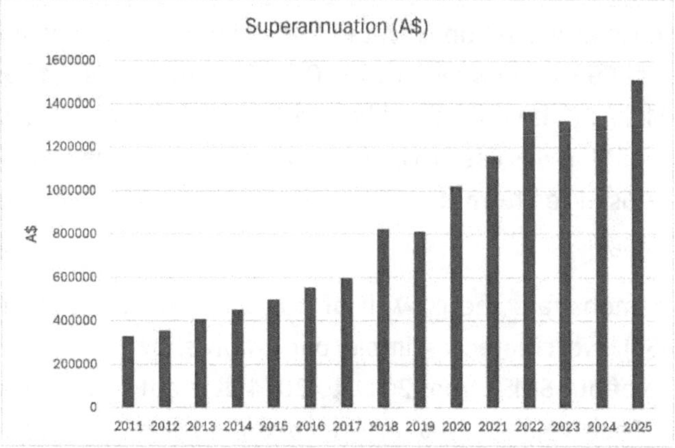

Figure 8: Superannuation growth between 2011 and 2025 for Mary and Ranjan Superfund

Starting in 2011 with A$328,000, our self-managed super fund (SMSF) grew to an impressive A$1.34 million by 2024. The graph shows a steady rise, with early gains past A$400,000 by 2014, a jump to A$600,000 by 2017, and a surge to A$1 million by 2021, peaking at A$1.5 million. Extra contributions beyond the compulsory 11% super guarantee, paired with smart investments, drove this growth. The steep climb from 2019 suggests market gains and strategic moves turned our fund into a seven-figure success.

Our SMSF journey is not about bragging—it is about showing what is possible with a bit of patience and planning. We did not earn millions overnight or strike it rich in crypto. We simply made regular extra contributions, invested wisely, and let time do the rest.

Reaching A$1.5 million in super was a huge milestone for us. It represents not just money, but the freedom to retire on our own terms, help our family, and not worry about every dollar in our later years.

Some people think super is boring, locked away, or just a "later in life" problem. But for us, it became a silent wealth builder that grew steadily in the background while we went about our lives. For those of you wondering where to start, consider this: superannuation is one of the most tax-friendly, long-term wealth-building tools Australians have. And if you are ready to take more control, an SMSF might just be your quiet millionaire-maker too.

Shop around for insurances

Every year, we must renew three cars and 5 real estate properties that need annual insurances. Every year when a renewal comes, we noticed that the amounts are increased $200-500 on each policy. We worked out if we did not get new quotes each year, we will be spending extra approximately $2000 per year, which over 25 years becomes a **significant saving of $50,000**. Comparing new quotes is quick and easy by going to various websites. If you are switching from insurer to another, we find that there is always a discount. I can give a recent example for home and content insurance for our home, which was quoted as approximately $2000 but when I got an alternative quote, it came of approximately $1500 per year. These small savings are part our strategy of slow spending.

We know some people get overwhelmed by the idea of managing all these policies and keeping track of renewal dates. But honestly, it's not that bad. We use a simple spreadsheet to keep everything organized. We just list out each car and property, the insurance company, the renewal date, and how much we paid last year. That way, when a renewal is coming up, we can see briefly if the price has jumped and whether it is time to start shopping around again.

And here is another tip: do not be afraid to negotiate with your current insurer. If you find a cheaper quote somewhere else, call up your existing company and let them know. Sometimes, they will match the lower price or even beat it to keep your business. It does not always work, but it's worth a try. The worst they can say is no, and then you just switch to the cheaper option.

This whole process has become a bit of a routine for us now. It is just part of our annual financial check-up, like reviewing our budget or checking our investments. It does not take much time, and the savings are totally worth it. Plus, it feels good to know we are not getting ripped off just for being lazy or sticking with the same company out of habit.

We think a lot of people just accept these price increases because they do not realize there are better options out there, or they think it is too much hassle to switch. But it is one of the easiest ways to save a chunk of money every year without making any real sacrifices. You still get the coverage you need, but you are not paying more than you must.

General sacrifices

Looking back at our lifestyles, we have noticed that we were following the slow spending strategy in our daily routines. Here are some examples that come to mind.

While working in Sydney for 6 years, which is an hour flight from Melbourne, it was a very hectic schedule for us. This involved every Monday, Mary getting up at 4 AM, packing lunch, driving to the airport in Melbourne, taking two local trains in Sydney and getting to work at 8AM. Then there was same routine every Friday back to Melbourne. It was highly inconvenient to wake up at 4AM every morning and taking 6AM flight from Melbourne to Sydney on Mondays and returning Friday evening week after week for 6 years but that was a sacrifice that we were prepared to do.

While in Sydney, she chose to rent a room with a friend rather than moving into own apartment, we had already purchased. Sharing a house for Mary in Sydney with another person was not only cheap but also led to a log term friendship with the owners of the house.

Many times, while both working and children at school, our house has been a mess, and we have thought of having someone to come and clean the house. Some of our friends have had someone coming once a week to deep clean-up of the house, so their house will look very tidy compared to ours. But we had other goals on top of our list, such as paying off the investment properties and saving for trips to India and Ireland where our parents lived.

Mary and I have mostly bought non-branded clothes and shoes. We believe that if the quality and comfort are good, we do not need any branding. At the same time, this has allowed us to buy branded clothes and shoes for our children.

Most of our earlier periods (up 50 years age) we did not have paid TV channels such as Foxtel. At work, people will discuss how proud they were to have Foxtel, but we were simply happy with free-to-air channels.

For about 25 years Mary used a hairdresser running a business from home and saved at least $50 per visit. With average six visit per year, over 25 years, this comes to **A$7,500**.

For over 20-year ranjan used a barber running a business from home and charged $8 per visit as compared to $15 charged by other low-cost barbers, thus saving six visits per year, saving $7 per year with total $140 in 20 years). For last 10 year, as gradually lost his hair, he has been using an electric head shaver that cost $150.

While raising the babies in New Zealand we mostly used cloth nappies as the diapers were quite expensive.

Buying a property rather than renting

For some reasons, we always thought that we should own our own place as soon as possible. In the end property investment has been the biggest contributor to our financial health. We have bought properties within and outside or superannuation fund.

As a student at Massey University, New Zealand in 1989-93, Ranjan rented at various places in Palmerston North as he was on a scholarship of NZ$800-$1,000 per month. Ranjan supplemented his income by cleaning staff tearoom and supervising laboratory which added another $50-60 per week to his income. The aim was to spend minimum on rents, so had to keep moving and finding cheaper accommodation. Luckily, the rent for a room in a shared house in New Zealand was low ($50-55 per week). When Ranjan met Mary and they moved together, they found one-bedroom small unit that was quite cost effective with a rent of $110 per week.

When we got married in March 1994, we were 31 and 29 years old, continued to rent the small unit but also started looking for a home to have a family. At that time, we had almost no savings and the house prices in Palmerston North town, where we lived were between NZ$140,000-200,0000. With modest salary of approximately NZ $35,000/year each (before tax), we thought that the prices were too high. So, we started looking outside the town and found a country house for NZ$105,000 in a place called Bunnythorpe, about 8 km from our work. As we could only afford 5% deposit, we only had limited funding opportunities. We first approached the Trust Bank in New Zealand but could not secure a mortgage. The bank did consider us a safe investment for lending money even though both had long-term employment. Ultimately, Bank of New Zealand offered us loan of $91,800 at the interest rate of 7.4%. We also had to fork out $1539 for fee and insurance.

At the time when we moved to Denmark in 1999, we had not realised that our stay would be short (~1.5 years). Still, after renting for 6 months, we bought a small apartment of our own in Copenhagen. We were able to sell as well in early 2001 when we moved to Australia when Ranjan got a job offer from CSIRO, Werribee.

When in February 2001 we landed in Australia with two kids (1.5 and 4.5 years old) we had approximately A$170,000 in our savings total with no debt. We looked around for houses in our area (near Ranjan's work). We rented for 6 months than bought a home with cash within our budget. When we bought our first house in Australia in late 2001, it felt like we were signing our lives away. We bought a three-bedroom house for A$148,000 paid full in cash. In 2008, we upgraded to a bigger house with a pool for children for A$450,000. Fast forward 20 years, and the financial benefits of owning are crystal clear. That first house, which we paid A$450,000 for, is now worth over A$1 million.

Property investment - our pathway to become millionaires

In this section we present our property investment journey which has been full of ups and downs and ultimately formed pathway to become millionaires. With our habits of **slow spending**, as we scrimped and saved, we were able to make extra payments to property loans. The extra payments, no doubt accelerated the time we took to become mortgage free.

Here is our journey of property investment starting from New Zealand.

New Zealand

Our first ever home in New Zealand – not a great investment

We bought this home (or first home) in May 1994 for NZ$102,000 and sold with great difficulty for NZ$104,000 in 2000 (it was very hard selling a house then!). Despite living for 5 years and refurbishing the house with new flooring, curtains and wallpaper, we did not make any money on the

house. This experience taught us that price depends on

demand and supply. In Palmerston North, the demand was too low at the time. However, we do have sweet memories of the place as both our children were born there.

After that experience, we were determined to pay off the home loan as soon as we could. We remember that we were mortgage and debt free in just over 4 years. In a way, that was a stepping stone for our desire to stay debt free later in life. In a way, we were lucky that both of us were employed and through our frugal habits were heavily focused on repaying the mortgage.

What lessons did we learn from our first ever property purchase? We think that owning this modest home gave us the feeling of real freedom and showed us how to be financially disciplined. This was also a stepping stone in what we call now, "**the slow spending**" which encapsulates spending considerably lower than earnings and investing heavily.

Denmark

We worked in New Zealand until 1999 when we took an opportunity to work in Denmark. With two boys 3.5 years and 6 months old, we moved to Copenhagen, Denmark where Ranjan got a job the at the Royal Agricultural and Veterinary University (KVL). Mary also joined the same place as research scientist at a later stage.

Initially, we rented an apartment in Copenhagen, but we really wanted to have our own place. Fortunately, we were able to buy a small 2-bedroom apartment (64m^2 plus a small balcony), which was within our budget. We always knew that we were not big spenders, although the apartment being quite small, we learnt to enjoy the place. In fact, being in Copenhagen, we had a flurry of visitors from New Zealand, Ireland, and India. We managed to share the small apartment happily with the visitors. By that time, we had developed a frugal lifestyle, which we later call **Slow Spending**, by shopping at cheap supermarkets such as Netto and Lidl.

Our apartment purchase in Denmark

We bought the apartment for DKK914,000 (~A$198,000) in 2000 and sold for DKK950,000 (A$206,000) after living about a year in the apartment. So, it was not a bad investment as we recovered all our costs, and we got to save on 1 year rental (~A$18,000).

Meget lys lejlighed med nyt køkken og nye hårde hvidevarer i veldrevet ejerforening - ***mulig delelejlighed***

Emne: Ejerlejlighed		EDC nr.:	20157156
Beliggenhed: Ane Katrines Vej 26, 3.th 2000 Frederiksberg		Boligareal:	64
		Grundareal:	0
Kontantpris :	892.000	Antal værelser:	3
Finansieret pris:	914.000	Mdl. bruttoydelse:	7.402
Udbetaling:	55.000	Mdl. nettoydelse:	6.024

What lessons we learnt from our investment in Denmark? Although, we were in Denmark for a short period (1.5 years), we learnt that buying a place was still profitable than just renting. We also created memories that will last with us forever.

Although the lifestyle in Denmark was good, we loved the people and the country, we also struggled with the language (especially Ranjan). In early 2001, Ranjan got a job offer from Australia's premium research organisation, CSIRO, which we could not resist. CSIRO offered to pay relocation for the family to Australia. So, with older son being 4.5 and the younger one being 1.5 years old, we again packed up and left Denmark to Australia.

Australia

February 2001, when we stepped off the plane in Melbourne, the air smelled different—crisp, full of promise. Mary and I were wide-eyed, clutching our suitcases and our dreams of a new life. With two young kids in tow, we did not have much, but we had enough to start with total savings of A$170,000. For the first six months, we rented a modest three-bedroom unit in Werribee. It was cozy, but it was not ours. The landlord was decent, but every creaky floorboard and peeling paint chip reminded us we were building someone else's wealth, not our own. That is when we decided to take the plunge and buy our first home in Australia.

Our investment property buying journey really started in Australia

As we have mentioned, immediately after arriving in Australia, we rented a house for 6 months then bought our fist property. It was always in our mind to buy as soon as possible once we are settled in Australia. When we arrived in Australia in February 2001, we had total savings of ~A$170,000. We knew that that was our total budget, and we always wanted to have some buffer in our account so not all the money was available for a house. We wanted to stay closer to Ranjan's work in CSIRO, Werribee, which is in the western suburbs of Melbourne. We did not spend a lot of time in searching. So, we found a 3-bedroom house in Hoppers Crossing, about 5 km from Ranjan's work. As our children were quite small (~2 and 5 years old), the property was quite convenient as there was also a primary school nearby (Cambridge Primary School).

The very first house that we bought cost us A$148,000 (plus $2000 disbursements). We bought that with cash and did not have to borrow. **At that stage Ranjan was 38 and Mary was 35 years old.**

August 2001 – our first foray into residential property

Our first home in Australia. It was a moderate 3-bedroom house. We bought this house at the age of 38 and 35 years for A$148,000 from our savings with no mortgage. As we paid the full amount in cash were able to negotiate the price making a saving of A$4,000. Also, as we did not have to borrow and it saved us $7,000 in lender's mortgage insurance. Thus, by having our funds to buy this property, we were able to **save A$11,000**.

What lessons we learnt from buying our first property in Australia? We learnt what steps were needed to buy a property in Australia. These included, property inspections, making an offer and negotiating a price, arranging a property conveyancer, paying deposit and arranging bank transfers for final payments. Further expenses included stamp duty paid to the state government and arranging house and content insurance. This experience was useful in our further property investments.

Commercial land – Altona – a beginner's mistake

June 2001 - After arriving in Australia, without carrying out any research we bought 1200 m^2 undeveloped commercial land in Altona, which was in one of the growing industrial suburbs of Melbourne. In May 2003, we paid A$62,000 for the land and sold it for A$125,000 in March 2025. Over 20 year, the property was never developed as there were several issues with the land, such as the presence of native flora and fauna which could not be disturbed without changing regulations which did not happen in our time. This land also cost us about A $400 per year for council and water rates, totally A$8,000 over 20 years. On the hind side, it was a bad investment because if we had

invested in a residential land for that price, it would have been about A$400,000 in 2025.

What lessons we learnt? A due diligence on the property and its potential for growth is essential, especially when buying a commercial property.

2005 – Commercial property off-the-plan

In December 2005, we came across an advertisement for a new development of units in a commercial area of Hoppers Crossing. We signed on for a unit **off the plan**. That cost us A$195,000 plus disbursements. We developed a dedicated laboratory design for the internal structure of the building with the aim of Ranjan starting a food research business. Having a dedicated laboratory allowed Ranjan to start his own company in food research later in life. We also invested over $150,000 further to expand the laboratory facilities. When Ranjan was not using the laboratory, the place was leased out and has now formed a constant source of revenue for us. The current value of the property is over $550,000.

When did we learn from this investment? As the property was bought off the plan and as were the first few investors, we were able to purchase the property at a discount rate as the builder needed people to sign agreement to get finance. Having a dedicated food research laboratory allowed Ranjan to run a profitable and a successful business and when Ranjan decided to retire in 2024, this property became a source of revenue that will only grow with time. There is always some risk when buying a property off the plan, we were lucky to have a good builder.

August 2008 - Our second home

We bought our upgraded home in August 2008, after staying for about 7 years in our first home. For this house we had to get some loan for from bank. The main attraction of the property was the large backyard and a swimming pool which at the time was quite attractive proposition as both our boys were keen swimmers.

The purchase price for this house was A$460,000 and we had to borrow $350,000 as we had not sold our first home at the time of purchasing this house. Once, the first house was sold we immediately paid off this house saving thousands of dollars in interest. Again, this case as we had over 20% deposit, we made savings on lender's mortgage insurance of **about $15,000**.

North Ipswich, Queensland – A small Mistake

At one stage Ranjan changed his employment and found a job at University or Queensland and Brisbane. At the beginning, Ranjan moved alone to Queensland while mary stayed in Melbourne with boys. We were fortunate to have a friend who put Ranjan up until he found a place to live. Again, we had no intention of renting, so we bought our own place in North Ipswich.

Maher Street, North Ipswich

Sold Tuesday 01-Dec-09

IMPRESSIVE LUSH GREEN 1395M2 PARCEL IN NORTH IPSWICH

Nestled in a quiet location is this rejuvenated home encased by landscaped established gardens with mango trees, pecan and macadamia nut trees - positioned to maximise privacy. Cleverly-designed the floor plan encompasses a total of 5 bedrooms - 3 bedrooms all with built-ins and ceiling fans upstairs (with the master bedroom [illegible], second bedroom having its own walk in robe), downstairs has another two bedrooms (5th bedroom can be used as a large entertaining area if desired).

Your covered pool side entertaining space is complete with built-in seating and tables which services your own private oasis featuring sun deck overlooking the in ground salt water [illegible] built pool (you know it's been built to last) and shade sails. Other standout features 22000 + 12000L water tanks, energy efficient lighting in all areas except kitchen dining, home theatre with speakers filtered through to the down stairs lounge and outside entertainment area, plantation shutters featured throughout the home. Fully security screen on all windows and doors, all locks keyed alike, two garden sheds, two car carport with [illegible] path leading to front door, upstairs patio.

We bought this property in December 2009 for A$448,000 of which we borrowed A$300,000 from BankWest meaning we had a 33% deposit (A$148,000). Having deposit of over 20% meant that we saved on lender's mortgage insurance which otherwise costs 2 to 5% of the loan amount. If we only had 5% deposit, we would be looking at additional cost of up to A$20,000 in lender's mortgage insurance. It should be noted that this insurance only covers the lender, one still needs to get mortgage protection insurance.

We had this property rented out for about 7 years. Although the rental income initially was good (gross ~4%), gradually we stated getting poor tenants and we found it hard to sell the property as the market was quite slow.

Ultimately, the property was sold in June 2018 for A$445,000. This property was one of the worst investments that we had made. At the time market was quite slow, we were having troubles with tenants, we had to sell it off at a loss. We lost about $5,000 in the transactions on this property. As the property had several maintenance issues, we were relieved to get rid of the property.

What lessons we learnt from this investment? The location of a property is extremely important as it determines the growth potential and ease of exit when selling. Another lesson we learnt was that if property is not selling, holding it for a longer period can be beneficial, as in this case the property did appreciate to near $750,000 in 2024.

Taringa, Brisbane – small profit

In December 2009, we purchase a small unit close to University of Queensland for A$361,000 with loan of A278,000. As we had a deposit of over 20% ($83,000), we **saved on the stamp duty of A$10,000**. Although Ranjan was happily working in University of Queensland, Mary found it very hard to find suitable employment in Queensland. As the children were still small and were not keen on relocating to Queensland, Ranjan decided to come back to Melbourne and joined a Dairy Research Organisation in 2010. We off-loaded the apartment August 2015 for A$385,000 as we had difficulties in getting decent tenants. This unit made a **small profit of about A$20,000**.

What lessons we learnt from this property? It was our first foray into buying an apartment in Australia, we learnt a lot in terms of the costs of maintaining an apartment in Australia. We learnt that apart from the usual costs, such as water and council rates, we needed to fork out so called, "body corporate fee" which is common fund needed to maintain the building and surroundings. The body corporate fee can be very high as take up as much as third of the rental income.

Rydalmere, Sydney – beginning of successful property investment journey

In 2013, Mary got an opportunity to work in Sydney for a large Australian food company. As usual, we started looking for a property in Sydney. We found an off-the-plan, 3-bedroom apartment in a suburb called Rydalmere. Rydalmere is well connected by bus and river ferry services to the CBD Sydney. The property was on a design stage and offered off the plan for sale.

In Australia, off the plan property is offered by a builder when the builder has a new project design that needs investors. In such properties, the purchaser pays concessional stamp duty. The savings can be large depending on the price of the property.

The property price was A $520,000; we were able to negotiate to A$515,000 and the buying process involved a deposit of 10% of the property and rest paid on completion of the property. We liked the design and paid the deposit in April 2013. The building had 9 apartments, and our apartment was on the ground floor.

We had never purchased a property off the plan before. There was a significant risk in case the property was not completed, or the builder went financially bankrupt.

During the construction of the building, the builder provided us regular updates on the progress of the building.

Overall, we were very impressed by the sales agent and communications from the builder. Once, the building was completed, we were also impressed with quality of the fittings and furnishings. The apartment was initially rented out once completed for $550 per week. Of course, the rent kept increasing over time.

Although the aim of buying this apartment in Rydalmere was for Mary to live it, she did not want to stay alone in the apartment. She managed to find a room in furnished house of a friend. The rental for the room was significantly lower ($200 per week) than the rental of the new apartment ($560 per week). Over 6 years that **saved us approximately A$108,000**, which helped to pay off the loans faster than expected.

Rydalmere, Sydney – another successful property investment

In July 2014, the real estate agent informed us that the same builder was planning to build another set of apartment and asked if we wanted to invest. We were so impressed with the builder; we did not hesitate this time. The apartment in Rydalmere itself and was of the same specification as our first apartment (3 bedrooms, 2 bathroom and 2 car parks) but was priced at A$600,000. There was total 12 apartments in the complex. Again, we paid the deposit (A$60,000) and waited for the completion of the apartment. The building was completed in October 2015, and we rented the apartment for A$560 per week.

What lessons we learnt? As we bought both the properties in Rydalmere off the plan, we were able to save on stamp duty and get discounts on purchases. One needs to keep in mind that such purchases could go wrong as some builders are unable to complete the constructions due to various reason, sometimes beyond their control. Buying a brand-new property meant that we were able to find tenants easily and needed little and no maintenance over time. From the financial point of view, buying a new property is beneficial as the depreciations are significantly higher for a new property then in an old property.

Properties bought under superannuation fund

As we discuss later, we set up as self-managing superfund (SMSF) in February 2011. We used the funds in the SMSF to buy a couple of properties.

Melbourne CBD office

As a part of our self-managed superfund, at one stage we bought an office unit in Melbourne CBD for A$ 230,000 Sold for A$251,000 in August 2018, after holding for 7 years. This was not a great investment as we struggled to find a tenant once the original tenant vacated the property.

What lessons we learnt? We found that there was surplus supply of office space in the Melbourne CBD and one needs to do due diligence before getting into office properties.

Hoppers Crossing – sound location close to train station

We bought this property for A$300,000 in May 2013 for a bank loan of A$216,000 having rest as the deposit. This property was rented immediately and currently forms a portfolio of income for our superannuation fund. We saw poor rental but a good capital growth of the property, being valued at $650,000 in 2026.

What lessons we learnt? Having a property with a good location is beneficial and helps in growing the property value. However, another lesson we learnt was that an old property needs constant maintenance. This property has cost us a fair bit in repairing bathroom, replacing appliances, updating fire safety *etc*.

Corio – a property with future growth potential

In February 2023, when we had sufficient funds in our superannuation account, we purchased another property for A$435,000 with no bank loan in Corio. The property is next to the main road, we believe the property will appreciate with time. In June 2026, the property was valued at A$600,00 showing a modest increase in value.

What lessons we learnt? Again, this property being old has resulted in significant expenses including replacing dishwasher, bathroom fittings, and replacing the fence. However, we believe that this property is good long-term investment.

India

A building project in India

Although we did not buy a property for investment in India, we have constructed a building on an ancestral land owned by Ranjan as a potential social enterprise.

The building is partially completed with a portion already rented out. We are gradually spending money on improving this property and this property does not make us any money! This is a conscious decision on our part as we believe that we have been fortunate and have decided to give something back to the community. Our long-term aim of this project in India is generating enough income to support local community through guidance, training and education of rural youths, girls, and females.

At the time of authoring this book, India property is on-going project.

What have we learnt from this investment? Building construction in India can be expensive and take a long time and one needs to be patient.

Our tips for property investment

One of the advantage of owning a property in Australia is that no matter how much your primary residence is worth, there is no capital gains tax. Which means when you sell, you keep all the proceeds. Which is not the case with investment properties. Investment properties in Australia are taxed at the marginal rate of tax. So, whatever, tax bracket you are in that will be the rate for the capital gains on investment properties. If you hold the investment property for more than a year, the tax is applied on only the 50% gain in property value (*in the latest federal budget in 2026, this discount is no longer available for property buyer from July 2027 and a minimum tax of 30% will be applied from any capital gains*).

Our advice is to get into property as soon as possible – At the beginning, it may not seem like a good financial decision, and you may think that you are unable to finance one. Below are our thoughts to address the some of the issues that may come across while deciding to invest in properties.

- **Not able to find a lender at a young age** – this is where you may leverage on parents and relatives, if they are able to support. Alternatively, you may have to choose lenders that may lend you but at a higher interest rate. That is fine, but you should make sure that you have flexibility to change lenders without little or no fees. If that is the case, once you have a loan and have some repayment history (1-2 years), you will find that there are many banks that will let you switch to them.

- **Income too low** – In that situation, once you have loan approved, consider sharing rooms of the house. If you buy a 3-bedroom house, consider renting out 2 bedrooms. You may be able to easily offset 50-60% of your mortgage payment. Remember, there are sacrifices needed when **slow spending** (i.e. spending at a slower rate than income). We believe this situation will change in 5-6 year.
- **Don't want to be tied up for 25-30 years loan** – This seems like a long period to commit, however, as we have found, it disciplines us from day as you see a compulsory, large monthly repayment. You work around other expenses to make sure that payment is made each month. If there were no mortgage, as humans we tend to spend any spare money without much consideration. This repayment period is considerably shortened if you can repay the loan faster.
- **You are better off investing the cash in share market and get better returns than property investment** – That may be true, however, share market is not for everyone. People lose money in share market. If you are not repaying mortgage, which compulsorily forces you to save, you must be highly disciplined so that you save money for the share market. With so many temptation on spending, it can be daunting to be disciplined in saving. Have investment loans made us highly financially disciplined and motivated to focus on loan repayments.
- **You are not tied to one place and can move freely if the life and job situations change** – that may be true, but this fear should not stop you from buying. If you

need to change job or location, you have an ability to rent the whole place out. In that case the rent will generally cover 70-80% of the mortgage repayment but you will have to pay rent yourself. Again, it makes you financially disciplined which is core basis of slow spending

Positive gearing than negative gearing

Just to explain, positive gearing happens when the rental income from your investment property is more than the expenses you fork out—like mortgage interest, maintenance, council rates, and property management fees. In other words, you are making a profit from day one and will pay tax on that profit, but it is a sign your property is working for you, not the other way around. Negative gearing, on the flip side, is when your expenses outstrip your rental income, so you are running at a loss. The upside? You can claim that loss as a tax deduction to reduce your taxable income in Australia. It is a strategy plenty of Aussies use, especially in a market like Australia where tax breaks can feel like a lifeline. This loophole has now been closed in the 2026 federal budget where negative gearing only allowed for new properties.

One massive advantage of positive gearing of properties for us was the immediate positive cash flow. When your property's bringing in more rent than it costs to maintain, you have got extra money hitting your bank account each month. Another big win for positive gearing is how it fast-tracks paying off your loans. With extra cash coming in, you can chuck more at your mortgage principal, knocking out that debt quicker. Negative gearing, by contrast, often relies on a long-term strategy of holding properties for capital growth while you are still in debt, sometimes for decades. If the market does not boom as expected, or if you hit a rough patch (say, a tenant leaves or rates spike), those ongoing losses can start to sting. Positive gearing gives you more control and less stress, as you are not constantly betting on future market gains to justify the red ink.

Then there is the psychological side. Owning properties that are positively geared feels empowering—you are not just hoping for a future payday; you are seeing results now. That steady income can give you confidence to expand your portfolio or take on other investments, knowing your properties are self-sustaining.

One thing to note is that positive gearing often works best in certain markets. Regional areas or outer suburbs in Australia, where property prices are lower but rental yields are higher, can be goldmines for positive gearing. High-demand areas like inner-city Sydney or Melbourne might lean toward negative gearing because sky-high prices make it tough to cover costs with rent alone. Your strategy likely involved picking the right properties—ones with strong rental returns relative to their purchase price—which has set you up for success.

For us, positive gearing has been the ticket to building wealth slowly and steadily, paying off properties faster, and now enjoying a sweet stream of rental income without the burden of debt. It is less about chasing tax breaks or banking on market booms and more about creating a sustainable, profitable portfolio. Our 25 years of experience prove it works—proof that sometimes the less flashy strategy is the one that gets you to the finish line with a smile.

Buying a house of moderate value

We have always tried to buy a house of moderate value rather than an extravagant house, be it our own home or an investment property. We never wanted to overstretch our budget when it came to investing in property. That means we could not buy in the most sought-after location where the property is more likely to grow faster than the other places. On some occasions we have struggled to recover what we had invested. For example, we lost money on own first home in New Zealand, an apartment in Brisbane and house in North Ipswich. On the hindside, holding on to the properties for a longer period would have been wiser, however, we also realised that by not selling at the time, we were restricting ourselves from buying in other places.

- Buying a more modest home frees up capital for investment properties, which can generate positive cash flow and improve your overall financial position.
- Higher value homes require larger mortgages and tie up more capital, potentially limiting your ability to invest elsewhere.
- Appreciation is influenced more by location and market conditions than by the initial purchase price alone.

- Investment properties can be self-sustaining if they generate positive cash flow, providing extra income and financial flexibility.

By carefully considering the trade-offs between a higher value home and a more modest one, one can optimize your capital for investment and improve your long-term cash flow and wealth.

Buying property off-the-plan

If possible, buy off the plan as it can save significant amount in stamp duty. Stamp duty imposed by the State governments in Australia, can be prohibitive, the amount ranging from $15,000 to over $60,000, depending on the price of the property. The apartments we bought in Sydney were off the plan, **saving us total $30,000**. It should be noted that there is an inherent risk in buying a property off the plan of losing the deposit if the builder goes bankrupt before the completion of the property.

Having minimum deposit to avoid lender's mortgage insurance

Always have enough deposit to avoid lender's mortgage insurance. In Australia, if you cannot have 20% deposit for a property loan, you are required to pay for lender's mortgage insurance, which only covers the lenders but not the borrowers. So, if for some reasons, the borrower in unable to service the loan, the lenders (banks) are covered by insurance. We believe we save approximately $4000 on each property, **overall saving of A$28,000**. Besides, having higher deposit helps in making a positively geared property which was our strategy.

Switching home loans to cheaper providers

When it comes to money matters, we have always believed in doing a bit of homework and not just sticking with the first option that comes our way. That approach really paid off when it came to our home loan.

Our first home loan was with AMP. At the time, we did not know much about how home loan rates varied from bank to bank. We were just happy to get a loan and buy our first home. But a few years in, we started noticing how even a small difference in interest rates could add up to a big chunk of money over time.

That's when we started looking around and came across Bankwest, which was offering a better deal. It was not a massive difference, but even saving half a percent meant we could either reduce our repayments or keep them the same and knock a few years off the loan term. So, we made the switch.

But the real gamechanger came around 2010. We heard about UBank – a new online bank launched by NAB with a focus on "self-directed" customers. Basically, you managed everything yourself online or over the phone, which suited us just fine. We were comfortable doing things digitally, and the best part - their interest rate was nearly 2% lower than what we were paying.

That caught our attention straight away. We did the math – a 2% difference on a home loan was not a pocket change. On a loan of, say, $800,000, that is around $16,000 a year in interest savings!

So, we moved our investment loans to UBank. The process was straightforward – a bit of paperwork, a few phone calls, and it was done. From day one, the difference was obvious. We decided to keep paying the same amount we were paying before switching (which were significantly higher than minimum needed to service the loan), which meant more of our payment went toward the principal instead of interest. That small decision sped up our repayment plan significantly.

Over time, those interest savings gave us more breathing room. We could put more into our savings, make extra repayments, and feel more in control of our finances. It also gave us confidence – knowing we were not blindly handing over more money to the bank than we needed to.

Looking back, switching lenders a couple of times was one of the smartest financial decisions we made. It taught us not to be loyal to a bank just for the sake of it. Banks are businesses, and if we can get a better deal elsewhere, it makes sense to take it – especially when we are talking about long-term loans and serious money.

Have sole focus on repayment of property loans

Have a sole focus on repaying property investment loans: In our case, each month, we made sure we had enough to live on and some buffer for unforeseen circumstances, we transferred the funds as soon as they hit our accounts. We were paying sometime 3 or 4 times needed as a minimum payment per month. What this did this to our loans is that it not only reduced the principle fast but also the interest payments were getting lower as each instalment. When we were repaying property investment loans we did not think of buying anything substantial such as new furniture, clothes or shoe. We put off all renovations for home on hold until the loans were paid off. By the age of 55 for Ranjan and 52 for Mary, all our investment loans were paid off.

How we have enjoyed the benefits of slow spending?

Slow spending has taught us how to manage cashflow that empowers us to spend and enjoy without diluting out assets and net worth.

Although we have had disciplined spending throughout, we did take many opportunities to enjoy the benefits, especially regular overseas travels.

As we live in Australia and our folks live in Ireland and India, we have made several visits since marriage and after the birth of the children. Until very recently, we were planning our overseas holidays around the visit to India and Ireland. For example, while going to India we will choose different stopovers such as Malaysia, Thailand, Singapore or Vietnam and allow ourselves to spend a week or in these countries. Similarly, while going to Ireland, we have stopped for holidays in Dubai, Amsterdam, China. Having these breaks, as part of our travels to our folks in Ireland and India have saved us thousands of dollars. Once you are tuned into **slow spending**, saving at each transaction becomes a second habit.

Examples of our ability to spend freely during our slow spending. As we have had good cashflow and no debt, all the spendings were made from our own savings.

- Bathrooms renovations - $60,000
- Kitchen renovation - $50,000.
- New house doors - $11,000.

- Upgrade of power 3-phase supply - $6000
- Security cameras, lights and fence gate - $20,000
- Frequent travels abroad - $100,000-$200,000
- Solar panels and battery – $40,000
- House painting, curtains etc - $20,000
- Updating shed and swimming pool equipment - $15,000
- Buying 4 new cars using cash - $160,000

Apart from these large expenses, over many years, Ranjan has been regularly able to send small amounts of money back to India to his parents for several years and support their visits to New Zealand, Denmark and Australia.

Beijing, China and Liverpool, UK

Japan, Spain and Thailand

Houston, USA and Ireland

Cape Town, South Africa and Singapore

Benefits of financially savvy children

One of the proudest outcomes of our "**slow spending**" lifestyle has been how naturally it has rubbed off on our two sons. As parents, we did not preach too much about money—we just lived our lives being mindful of spending, saving carefully, and avoiding waste. We supported our children paying their private school and university fees. Over the years, without setting out to "train" our boys, they picked up on our habits. And now, we can clearly see how those small lessons have shaped their thinking and behaviour around money.

In our household, we have embraced a way of living that we call "slow spending." It is not about pinching pennies or denying ourselves the things we love. Instead, it is about being thoughtful with our money, prioritizing what truly matters, and teaching our two boys to do the same. Over the years, we have watched this mindset take root in their lives, shaping how they view possessions, money, and the world around them. It has been a journey, and we are proud to see how our values have influenced them in practical, down-to-earth ways that any family can relate to.

Slow spending, for us, means resisting the urge to chase after the latest trends or shiny new gadgets. It is about asking, "Do we really need this?" before making a purchase and finding joy in what we already have. We are an ordinary family, not wealthy by any stretch, but we have found that this approach has given us financial breathing room and a sense of contentment that's hard to put a price on. Our boys, now young adults, have picked up on this, and it is heartwarming to see how they have made it their own.

Take our older son, for example. He is in his late-20s now and living in a shared apartment in the heart of Melbourne's CBD. He could have chased after a fancy place with all the modern trimmings, but instead, he chose something affordable that suits his needs. Most of his furniture came from us—hand-me-downs like our old couch, a sturdy dining table, TV and a bed frame that has been in the family for years. He is perfectly happy with these second-hand pieces, and you would never hear him complain about them not being brand-new. In fact, he has taken the idea of slow spending even further. Instead of splurging on the latest smartphone or trendy clothes, he sticks to a budget-friendly mobile plan and wears the same reliable jackets and shoes he has had for years. They are still in good shape, so why replace them?

Living in the city, he has also embraced a lifestyle that does not rely on owning a car. Melbourne's trams, trains, and buses get him where he needs to go, and if it is close enough, he will walk. It is not just about saving money—though that is a big part of it—it's about living simply and reducing his environmental footprint. He is not preachy about it, but you can tell he is proud of the choices he has made. What is even more impressive is how he has taken the money he saves and put it to work. He has gotten into investing, dipping his toes into domestic and international shares. It is not something we pushed him into; he just saw the value in building for the future rather than spending everything he earns. Watching him research companies and make thoughtful investment choices feels like a win for us as parents. It shows he is not just avoiding unnecessary spending but actively planning for a stable future.

Our younger son, who is still living at home with us (at the time of writing the book), has taken a different but equally practical approach to slow spending. He is in his mid-20s, working a steady job, and because he is staying with us, his expenses are minimal. Rent-free living means he can save most of his paycheck, and he has been diligent about it. He is not one for flashy purchases either—no new gaming consoles, designer clothes, or expensive nights out. Instead, he is content with what he has and focuses on building a nest egg. When we talk about money as a family, he is the one asking questions about savings accounts and how to make his money grow over time. It is clear he has internalized the idea that wealth is not about what you show off but what you hold onto for the long haul. Following his brother's footsteps he has started investing in Australian and US stock markets.

For us, as parents, seeing our boys adopt these habits is a source of pride, but it has not always been easy to instil them. When they were younger, there were moments when they would see their friends with the latest sneakers or the newest phone and feel the pressure to keep up. We'd have open conversations about why we do not always buy the "next big thing." We would explain that companies are always trying to convince us we need something new, but most of the time, what we have is good enough. Over time, those talks stuck. We also made a point to lead by example—whether it was repairing an old appliance instead of replacing it or choosing second-hand furniture for our home. The boys saw us living these values, and it became normal for them.

In the end, we believe that slow spending is not just a money-saving technique. It is a lifestyle and a mindset. And the best part is, it is contagious. We hope that as our boys continue their own paths, they will carry these values forward—and maybe even pass them on to their own families one day.

Our Household net worth

Our household total net worth represents the total value of assets (financial as well as non-financial) minus the total value of outstanding liabilities.

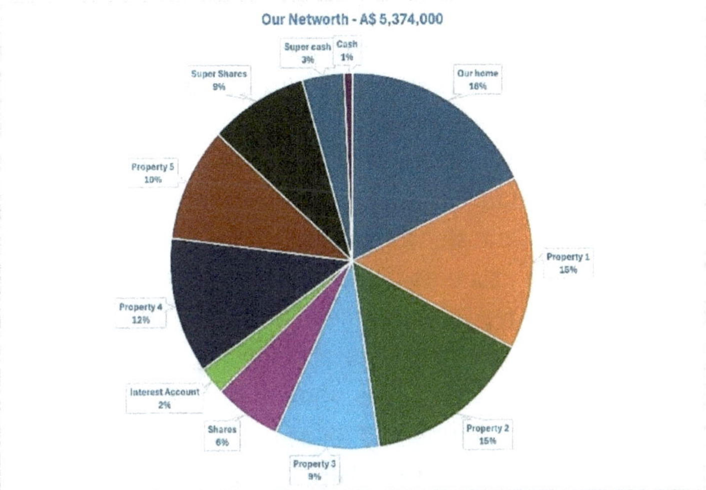

Figure 8: After 25 years for "slow spending our net worth in May 2026.

After 25+ years of following the strategy of "slow spending" we are proudly able to say that we have been debt free and financially secure for several years.

Lessons, regrets and final thoughts

Here is a summary what we think can help one become a millionaire by **slow spending**.

- Be educated and keep learning about investing and other financial tools. Many of the resources are available free on the Internet or local libraries.
- Always spend below your income and control your spending by slowing down any spending. Which means save heavily during the early stages of life. Practically, this means transferring a large chunk of your income to accounts that either bring down the debts or lead to investments and living off the balance. This may involve sacrificing on luxury items, buying in bulk, shopping groceries in cheaper supermarkets *etc*.
- Invest in an asset that forces you to save and requires compulsory tightening of belt. Our example is buying your own home and investing in property. Buy a house or an investment property if you do not own one and focus doggedly on paying the mortgage. Having a large debt trains us to be disciplined in our spending, focuses us on repayment of the investment loans and teaches us to optimise the income and expenses. We believe, unless you go through this rigorous

process, you cannot learn much about the value of money.

- While shopping or getting trade services, always look for discounts, whether its grocery or large items such as a car or hiring a plumber or electrician. In the case of buying a new car we have found that a demo car can save you thousands of dollars, yet it feels like a new car. If you like something, pause before you buy and sleep on the thoughts of buying. We have noticed that you follow this strategy, often, you often will forego that purchase. If you do need an essential item, such as a mobile phone, look for bargains on eBay or Amazon. Small savings over long period of time help the bottom line.
- In a partner/couple situation, pool the income through joint accounts and spend jointly. This reduces the wastage in managing two separate accounts and optimising the spending through one channel.

Overall, we believe, if you follow these rules, you may not become extremely wealthy but will sure become financially independent over a period of time. It is a slow process needing many years of slow spending but is less risky than many get rich quick schemes. Along the way you will learn, develop your own techniques for maximising savings and accumulate wealth. Your habit will no doubt be unknowingly embraced by your children.

A couple of areas that we could have done more was learning about share market earlier in our lives, focusing more on savings in superannuation and buying own dwelling in a sought-after location. Although, we did invest later in life in share market and made significant returns, early investments would have grown more than the growth of investment properties. We bought our home near Ranjan's work in an outer suburb of Melbourne. If we had bought in a more desired, inner suburb of Melbourne, it would have grown by another million dollars in past 20 years. Our property investments were limited to few properties only and did not take excessive mortgage. On the hindsight, we have realised that we could have leveraged on the equity built on the properties and borrowed more to invest in additional properties. In addition, earlier on in our property investment journey, we were too impatient to sell a couple of properties that became challenge due to poor returns, decline in property value and difficult tenants. The same properties have grown 50-60% in the past few years. Having said that, our aim always was to take manageable financial risks and not have sleepless nights due to financial worries.

As we are in early sixties, we believe that now we can focus on things in life that we have been postponing. We are planning to travel around the world. Again, it will be "**slow spending**" project and will be funded through our investment income. We are also in an early stage of a community project in India that we believe that can financially sustain itself. Based in rural India, in the foothills of Himalayas, our project aims to aid local women and girls to help them become independent through training and entrepreneurship.

Acknowledgements

We would like to express our sincere gratitude to the remarkable advancements in artificial intelligence (AI) that played a valuable role in shaping this book. We wish to acknowledge Claude, ChatGPT, Grok, Perplexity, and Gemini. In addition to editing support, we also used AI-powered tools to create some of the illustrations and images featured throughout the book. These visuals brought life to our concepts and added another dimension to the storytelling.

While the thoughts, experiences, and values shared in this book are entirely our own, we are grateful to these AI tools for helping us present them in the clearest and most engaging way possible.

About the authors

Ranjan was born and raised in India. Having completed his schooling in a remote village in foothills of Himalayas, he was awarded a place in a degree in dairy science and technology in Gujarat state in the western part of India. After completing his degree, he worked briefly for a dairy company in the

northern state of Punjab. In the meantime, he was offered a prestigious Indian Council of Agricultural Research (ICAR) scholarship to carry out master's research back in the dairy science college in Gujarat. After completing his master's degree, he applied for a PhD position in food science in various universities around the world and was offered a place at Massey University, New Zealand. Ranjan arrived in Palmerston North, New Zealand in June 1989 to start his PhD. After a delay of few months, he was awarded the New Zealand Vice Chancellor's research scholarship for his PhD.

Mary was born and raised in a small town, Midleton in County Cork in Ireland. After completing her master's degree in food science, she was awarded a Rotary scholarship for research in food science for 1 year. The scholarship was available for her to use in either USA or New Zealand, depending on where she could find a research position. She chose New Zealand and landed in Massey University in 1991.

Mary and Ranjan were married in 1994. They have two boys. They divide their time between India and Australia with occasional visits to Ireland. We plan to travel globally once Mary decides to leave her full-time employment in the very near future.